SELECTED ESSAYS

SELECTED ESSAYS

(FIRST SERIES)

by

SIR EDMUND GOSSE

Essay Index Reprint Series

BOOKS FOR LIBRARIES PRESS
FREEPORT, NEW YORK

73-14

First Published 1928
Reprinted 1968

LIBRARY OF CONGRESS CATALOG CARD NUMBER:
68-29210

PRINTED IN THE UNITED STATES OF AMERICA

PREFACE

IN the seraglio of Haroun al Raschid there was carved a list of the thirty physical perfections without all of which no woman could be considered beautiful. Some of our intellectual teachers, and especially the youngest of them, seem to apply a like stringent test to literature. If a work, of the past or the present, does not fulfil their exact demand, they will have none of it, and they declare Dickens unreadable because his novels are unlike those of Jane Austen, and Pope no poet because he has not the romantic wealth of Keats. So far from demanding thirty perfections from their mistress, they despise her if she has more than the one which they prefer.

Looking over the essays which have been selected for the Travellers' Library from my critical production of half a century, I think I may dare to say of myself that I have never been the dupe of this schismatic error. All my life long I have been wandering in the gardens of Armida, never rejecting the rose because it was not a jasmine, and never denying the beauty of orchids because they were not daisies. So much will I dare to say in my own defence now, in the twilight of my career,—I have

5

been consistent in the pursuit of what I felt to be excellence in every field of writing, without regard to prejudice or fashion. Let me claim for this catholicity what credit it deserves.

When I began to contemplate masterpieces, they were far from being subjected to the investigation which they receive to-day. Our youthful students do not appreciate their blessings. How would they like to go back to a time when a horrible paper-bound volume called *Dick's Shakespeare* was welcomed because there was no other cheap edition of the Bard on the market ? What would be their feelings to be told that there was no Shelley, no Coleridge, no Chaucer, no minor Elizabethan dramatist to be had complete, or even decently edited, for love or money ? The advance in this respect has been prodigious, it has even, in some instances, gone beyond the limits of what is reasonable. In my childhood there were no re-prints of various English classics of which there are now too many. But this latter-day profusion is a fault on the right side. It responds to a phenomenon which was not even dreamed of when I began to be a critic, namely, the intrusion of English Literature into the curriculum of juvenile study.

Of the merits of this particular change I will not say anything here, because I could not do so without prejudice to my private opinion. I must, however, acknowledge that the essays selected for these two volumes have no didactic purpose. They were not written, and they are not re-issued, for purposes of instruction. There is a sense, of course, in which all statements of fact are liable to instruct the reader who comes to them for positive information. But my object has never been to teach. I have not the peculiar gift which the teacher needs. Let me say quite clearly that I have always been an artist and never a tutor. From an accident in my temperament for which I can give no reason, since my childhood I have been like the unhappy Emperor Julian, who also was not fitted to teach. As it was in his case, so in mine there has possessed me, *incidit desiderium*, an intense love of books and of the history of authors. The indulgence of this passion has been the joy of my life, and my work as a critic is the result. It must be reflected, I think, in these Selected Essays. They represent my irresistible desire to share with others the infinite pleasures which literature has afforded me. And all I have ever hoped to do was to unlock one or two of the magical chambers in the palace of Haroun al Raschid.

EDMUND GOSSE.

May 1928.

7

CONTENTS

ON FLUCTUATIONS OF TASTE

ON FLUCTUATIONS OF TASTE

WHEN Voltaire sat down to write a book on Epic Poetry, he dedicated his first chapter to " Differences of Taste in Nations." A critic of to-day might well find it necessary, on the threshold of a general inquiry, to expatiate on " Differences of Taste in Generations." Changes of standard in the arts are always taking place, but it is only with advancing years, perhaps, that we begin to be embarrassed by the recurrence of them. In early youth we fight for the new forms of art, for the new æsthetic shibboleths, and in that happy ardour of battle we have no time or inclination to regret the demigods whom we dispossess. But the years glide on, and, behold ! one morning, we wake up to find our own predilections treated with contempt, and the objects of our own idolatry consigned to the waste-paper basket. Then the matter becomes serious, and we must either go on struggling for a cause inevitably lost, or we must give up the whole matter in indifference. This week I read, over the signature of a very clever and very popular literary character of our day, the remark that Wordsworth's was " a genteel mind of the third rank." I put down the newspaper in which this airy dictum was printed, and, for the

first time, I was glad that poor Mr. Matthew
Arnold was no longer with us. But, of course, the
evolutions of taste must go on, whether they hurt
the living and the dead, or no.

Is there, then, no such thing as a permanent
element of poetic beauty ? The curious fact is
that leading critics in each successive generation
are united in believing that there is, and that the
reigning favourite conforms to it. The life of a
reputation is like the life of a plant, and seems, in
these days, to be like the life of an animal. We
watch the seed, admiration for Wordsworth,
planted about 1795, shoot obscurely from the
ground, and gradually clothe itself with leaves till
about 1840; then it bursts into blossom of
rapturous praise, and about 1870 is hung with
clusters of the fruit of "permanent" appreciation.
In 1919, little more than a century from its first
evolution in obscurity, it recedes again in the
raggedness of obloquy, and cumbers the earth, as
dim old "genteel" Wordsworth, whom we are
assured that nobody reads. But why were "the
best judges" scornful in 1800 and again in 1919
of what gave the noblest and the most inspiriting
pleasure to "the best judges" in 1870 ? The
execution of the verse has not altered, the conditions of imagination seem the same, why then is
the estimate always changing ? Is every form of
poetic taste, is all trained enjoyment of poetry
merely a graduated illusion which goes up and
down like a wave of the sea and carries "the best
judges" with it ? If not, who is right, and who

is wrong, and what is the use of dogmatising ? Let us unite to quit all vain ambition, and prefer the jangle of the music-halls, with its direct " æsthetic thrill."

So far as I know, the only philosopher who has dared to face this problem is Mr. Balfour, in the brilliant second chapter of his *Foundations of Belief*. He has there asked, " Is there any fixed and permanent element in beauty ? " The result of his inquiry is disconcerting ; after much discussion he decides that there is not. Mr. Balfour deals, in particular, with only two forms of art, Music and Dress, but he tacitly includes the others with them. It is certain that the result of his investigations is the singularly stultifying one that we are not permitted to expect " permanent relations " in or behind the feeling of poetic beauty, which may be indifferently awakened by Blake to-day and by Hayley to-morrow. If the critic says that the verse of Blake is beautiful and that of Hayley is not, he merely " expounds case-made law." The result seems to be that no canons of taste exist ; that what are called " laws " of style are enacted only for those who make them, and for those whom the makers can bully into accepting their legislation, a new generation of law-breakers being perfectly free to repeal the code. Southey yesterday and Keats to-day ; why not Southey again to-morrow, or perhaps Tupper ? Such is the cynical *cul - de - sac* into which the logic of a philosopher drives us.

We have had in France an example of *volte-face*

in taste which I confess has left me gasping. I imagine that if Mr. Balfour was able to spare a moment from the consideration of fiscal reform, he must have spent it in triumphing over the fate of M. Sully-Prudhomme. In the month of September 1906 this poet closed, after a protracted agony, " that long disease, his life." He had compelled respect by his courage in the face of hopeless pain, and, one might suppose, some gratitude by the abundance of his benefactions. His career was more than blameless, it was singularly exemplary. Half-blind, half-paralysed, for a long time very poor, pious without fanaticism, patient, laborious, devoted to his friends, he seems to have been one of those extraordinary beings whose fortitude in the face of affliction knows no abatement. It would be ridiculous to quote any of these virtues as a reason for admiring the poetry of Sully-Prudhomme. I mention them merely to show that there was nothing in his personal temperament to arouse hatred or in his personal conditions to excuse envy. Nothing to account for the, doubtless, entirely sincere detestation which his poetry seemed to awaken in all " the best minds " directly he was dead.

As every one knows, from about 1870 to 1890, Sully - Prudhomme was, without a rival, the favourite living poet of the French. Victor Hugo was there, of course, until 1885—and posthumously until much later—but he was a god, and the object of idolatry. All who loved human poetry, the poetry of sweetness and light, took Sully-

Prudhomme to their heart of hearts. The *Stances et Poèmes* of 1865 had perhaps the warmest welcome that ever the work of a new poet had in France. Théophile Gautier instantly pounced upon *Le Vase Brisé* (since too-famous) and introduced it to a thousand school-girls. Sainte-Beuve, though grown old and languid, waked up to celebrate the psychology and the music of this new poetry, so delicate, fresh and transparent. An unknown beauty of extreme refinement seemed to have been created in it, a beauty made up of lucidity, pathos and sobriety. Readers who are now approaching seventy will not forget with what emotion they listened, for instance, to that dialogue between the long-dead father and the newly buried son, which closes :

> " J'ai laissé ma sœur et ma mère
> Et les beaux livres que j'ai lus ;
> Vous n'avez pas de bru, mon père,
> On m'a blessé, je n'aime plus."
>
> " De tes aïeux compte le nombre,
> Va baiser leurs fronts inconnus,
> Et viens faire ton lit dans l'ombre
> A côté des derniers venus.
>
> " Ne pleure pas, dors dans l'argile
> En espérant le grand reveil."
> " O père, qu'il est difficile
> De ne plus penser au soleil ! "

This body of verse, to which was presently added fresh collections—*Les Épreuves* (1886), *Les Vaines Tendresses* (1875), *Le Prisme* (1886),—was

17

welcomed by the elder Sanhedrim, and still more
vociferously and unanimously by the younger
priesthood of criticism. It pleased the superfine
amateurs of poetry, it was accepted with enthusiasm by the thousands who enjoy without
analysing their enjoyment. In 1880, to have
questioned that Sully - Prudhomme was a very
noble poet would have been like challenging
Tennyson in 1870, or Cowley in 1660. Jules
Lemaître claimed that he was the greatest artist
in symbols that France had ever produced.
Brunetière, so seldom moved by modern literature,
celebrated with ardour the author of *Les Vaines
Tendresses* as having succeeded better than any
other writer who had ever lived in translating into
perfect language the dawn and the twilight of
emotion. That Gaston Paris and M. Anatole
France competed in lofty praise of the lyrics of
Sully-Prudhomme, is perhaps less remarkable than
that Paul Verlaine, whom all the younger schools
still look upon as their apostle and guide, declared
in reviewing *Les Ecuries d'Augias*, that the force
of style of Sully-Prudhomme was excelled only by
the beauty of his detail. It is needless to multiply
examples of the unanimous praise given by the
divers schools of criticism to Sully - Prudhomme
up to about 1890. His was, perhaps, the least
contested literary glory of France.

His death startlingly reminded us that this
state of things had to be entirely reversed. It is
true that the peculiar talent of Sully-Prudhomme,
being almost exclusively lyrical, scarcely survived

his youth, and that he cumbered his moon of
sands with two huge and clumsy wrecks, *La
Justice* (1878) and *Le Bonheur* (1888), round
which the feet of the fairies could hardly be
expected to trip. One must be an academician
and hopelessly famous before one dares to inflict
two elephantine didactic epics on one's admirers.
Unfortunately, too, the poet undertook to teach
the art of verse in his *Réflexions* (1892) and his
Testament Poétique (1901), brochures which
greatly irritated the young. It is probably wise
for academicians, whether poets or the reverse, to
sit beside their nectar, and not to hurl bolts down
into the valley. But, behind these errors of
judgement, there they remain—those early volumes,
which seemed to us all so full of exquisite little
masterpieces. Why is it that nobody, except a few
elderly persons, any longer delights in them ? The
notices which Sully-Prudhomme's death awakened
in the Paris Press were either stamped with the
mark of old contemporary affection, or else, when
they were not abusive, were as frigid as the tomb
itself. " Ses tendresses sucrées, sirupeuses, sont
vaines en effet," said a critic of importance !
Indeed, it would appear so ; and where are the
laurels of yester-year ?

To those who were young when Sully-Prudhomme entered into his immortality it seems
impossible to realise that the glory has already
departed. Gaston Paris celebrated " the penetrating sincerity and the exquisite expression of
feeling " which distinguished Sully - Prudhomme

above all other poets. He was the bard of the inner life, sincere and dignified, full of melancholy reverie. A great critic compared *La Voie Lactée* and *Les Stalactites* with the far-off sound of bells heard down some lovely valley in a golden afternoon. Yet the images and the language were precise ; Sully-Prudhomme was a mathematician, and if he was reproached with anything like a fault, it was that his style was slightly geometrical. It would be otiose to collect any more tributes to his genius, as it appeared to all Frenchmen, cultivated or semi-cultivated, about the year 1880. With an analysis of Sully-Prudhomme's poetry I am not here concerned, but with the question of why it is that such an authority as Rémy de Gourmont could, in 1907, without awakening any protest among persons under fifty say that it was a " sort of social crime " to impose such balderdash as the verse of Sully-Prudhomme on the public.

It is not needful to quote other living critics, who may think such prolongation of their severities ungraceful. But a single contrast will suffice. When, in 1881, Sully-Prudhomme was elected to the French Academy, expert opinion throughout the Press was unanimous in admitting that this was an honour deservedly given to the best lyric poet of the age. In 1906, when a literary journal sent out this question, " Who is the poet you love best ? " and was answered by more than two hundred writers of verse, the diversity of opinion was indeed excessive ; such poets as Sainte-Beuve, as Brizeux, as Rodenbach received votes, all the great masters received many. But Sully-Prud-homme, alone, received not one vote. A new generation had arisen, and one of its leaders, with cruel wit, transferred to the reputation of the author his own most famous line : " N'y touchez pas, il est brisé."

It is necessary to recollect that we are not dealing with the phenomenon of the inability of very astute literary people to recognise at once a startling new sort of beauty. When Robert Browning lent the best poems of Keats to Mrs. Carlyle, she read them and returned them with the remark that " almost any young gentleman with a sweet tooth might be expected to write such things." Mrs. Carlyle was a very clever woman, but she was not quite " educated up to " Keats. The history of letters is full of these grotesque limitations of taste, in the presence of great art which has not yet been " classed." But we are here considering the much stranger and indeed extremely disconcerting case of a product which has been accepted, with acclamation, by the judges of one generation, and is contemptuously hooted out of court by the next. It is not, on this occasion, Sully-Prudhomme whom we are con-sidering, but his critics. If Théophile Gautier was right in 1867, Rémy de Gourmont must have been wrong in 1907 ; yet they both were honourable men in the world of criticism. Nor is it merely the *dictum* of a single man, which, however ingenious, may be paradoxical. It is worse than that ; it is the fact that one whole generation seems to have agreed with Gautier, and that another whole generation is of the same mind as Rémy de Gourmont.

Then it is that Mr. Balfour, like Galuppi with his " cold music," comes in and tells us that this is precisely what we have to expect. All beauty consists in the possession of certain relations, which being withdrawn, beauty disappears from the object that seemed to possess it. There is no permanent element in poetic excellence. We are not to demand any settled opinion about poetry. So Mr. Balfour seems to creak it, and we want the heart to scold. But is it quite so certain that there is no fixed norm of beauty imaginable ? Is it the fact that poetic pleasure cannot " be supposed to last any longer than the transient reaction between it " and the temporary prejudice of our senses ? If this be true, then are critics of all men most miserable.

Yet, deeply dejected as it leaves me to know that very clever people despise the " genteel third-rate mind " of Wordsworth, I am not quite certain that I yield to Mr. Balfour's brilliant and paralysing logic. That eminent philosopher seems to say " You find the poets, whom you revered in your youth, treated with contempt in your old age. Well ! It is very sad, and perhaps it would annoy me too, if I were not a philosopher. But it only shows how right I was to tell you not to expect permanent relations behind the feeling of beauty, since all is illusion, and there is no such thing as a principle of taste, but only a variation of fashion."

22

ON FLUCTUATIONS OF TASTE

Is it, however, quite so certain, after all, that there is no standard ? It must be admitted that there seems to be no fixed rule of taste, not even a uniformity of practice or general tendency to agreement in particular cases. But the whole study of the fine arts would lead to despair if we allowed ourselves to accept this admission as implying that no conceivable principle of taste exists. We may not be able to produce it, like a yard-measure, and submit works of imagination to it, once and for all, in the eyes of a consternated public. But when we observe, as we must allow, that art is no better at one age than at another, but only different ; that it is subject to modification, but certainly not to development ; may we not safely accept this stationary quality as a proof that there does exist, out of sight, unattained and un-attainable, a positive norm of poetic beauty ? We cannot define it, but in each generation all excellence must be the result of a relation to it. It is the moon, heavily wrapt up in clouds, and im-possible exactly to locate, yet revealed by the light it throws on distant portions of the sky. At all events, it appears to me that this is the only theory by which we can justify a continued interest in literature when it is attacked, now on one side, now on another, by the vicissitudes of fashion.

The essays which are here collected deal, for the most part, with figures in the history of English literature which have suffered from the changes of fortune and the instability of taste. In every case, there has been something which is calculated to attract the sympathy and interest of one who, like myself, has been closely concerned with two distinct but not unrelated branches of his subject, the literary character and the literary craft. More than fifty years have passed—like a cloud, like a dream!—since I first saw my name printed below a passage of critical opinion. How many reputations, within that half - century, have not been exalted, how many have not been depressed! We have seen Tennyson advanced beyond Virgil and Victor Hugo beyond Homer. We have seen the latest freak of futurism preferred to *The Lotus Eaters*, and the first *Légende des Siècles* rejected as unreadable. In face of this whirlwind of doctrine the public ceases to know whether it is on its head or its feet—" its trembling tent all topsy-turvy wheels," as an Elizabethan has it. To me it seems that security can only be found in an incessant exploration of the by-ways of literary history and analysis of the vagaries of literary character. To pursue this analysis and this exploration without bewilderment and without prejudice is to sum up the pleasures of a life devoted to books.

August 1919.

WALTER PATER

WALTER PATER

A PORTRAIT

FEW recent events can have surprised and saddened
the sincere lovers of literature more than the death,
in middle life, of Walter Pater. A peculiar vexa-
tion, so to speak, was added to the natural grief
such a loss must have caused, by the strange in-
exactitude, in matters of detail, which marked
almost all the notices of his career which appeared
at the time. In most of these notices, it is true,
there was manifested a wish to pay homage to
one of the most exquisite, the most self-respecting,
the most individual prose-writers of the age ; but
knowledge, especially of his earlier years and intellectual development, was lacking. He was one
who never had tempted the interviewer, who had
never chatted to the press about himself, and facts
regarding him were not at that abrupt moment
forthcoming.

How far accidents of time and place were
responsible for aiding this condition of things it
were now perhaps idle to speculate. The fame of
Walter Pater will not be wrecked on the holiday
of an editor or the indolence of a reporter. It is
grounded on the respect which has not yet failed
to follow pure and distinguished excellence in the
art of writing. As years go on, he will more and

more find his admirers, the rescuers of his renown. A subtle and penetrating essay by Mr. Lionel Johnson (in the *Fortnightly Review* for September 1894) has already pointed the way to those whose business it will be to detect Pater's influence upon his age, and to illustrate the individual merits of his style. In the following pages an attempt will be made to present the facts of the uneventful career of the author of *Marius*, so oddly travestied at the moment of his death, with some regard to continuity and truth. In preparing this sketch, I have had the encouragement and the help of the surviving members of his family, without whose co-operation I should not have undertaken such a task.

I

A very considerable interest attaches to the parentage of Walter Pater. His family was of Dutch extraction, his immediate ancestors having, it is believed, come over from the Low Countries with William of Orange. It was said, and our friend loved to believe it, that the court-painter, Jean Baptiste Pater, the pupil of Watteau, was of the same stock. If so, the relationship must have been collateral and not direct, for when the creator of so many delicate *fêtes champêtres* was painting in Flanders—he died in 1736—the English Paters had already settled at Olney, in Buckinghamshire, where they lived all through the eighteenth century. Reserved and shy, preserving many of their Dutch customs, they are described in family tradition as

28

mixing little with their neighbours, and as keeping through several generations this curious custom, that, while the sons were always brought up as Roman Catholics, the daughters were no less invariably trained in the Anglican faith. The father of Walter Pater quitted the Roman Church before his marriage, without adopting any other form of faith, and his two sons were the first Paters who were not brought up as Catholics.

Towards the close of the eighteenth century, the poet Cowper was the fellow-townsman and the friend of the Dutch emigrants in Olney, and the family long possessed some of his verses in his own manuscript. The son of the man who had known Cowper quitted the Buckinghamshire household, and went out to America. He settled in New York, associating chiefly with the Dutch colony in that city ; here his son, Richard Glode Pater, the father of the critic, was born. The family came back in the beginning of the present century, and settled at Shadwell, on the north shore of the Thames, between Wapping and Stepney, a situation now of extreme squalor, but eighty years ago still considered countrified and pleasant. Here, after his father's death, Richard Glode Pater continued to live, a medical practitioner working, mainly for the love of them, among poor folks in the East End, refusing to move into a more fashionable quarter, and despoiling himself of his patrimony by his constant benevolence.

To the house in Shadwell, Richard Glode Pater brought Maria Hill as his wife, and here were born to him four children, two of them sons, of whom Walter was the second. The elder son, William Thomson Pater, adopted his father's profession, and became the head of a large lunatic asylum. He died unmarried, on April 24, 1887, at the age of fifty-two, " quitting," in his brother's words, " a useful and happy life." In him, however, with the exception of a marked pleasure in being surrounded with pretty objects, not a single feature had ever shown itself of the peculiar intellectual characteristics or tastes of his brother. The future critic was born at Shadwell, on August 4, 1839, receiving the names of Walter Horatio, in compliment to a cousin who survives him.

Richard Glode Pater died so early that his second son scarcely remembered him in later life. The mother and grandmother left the house in Shadwell, and went to live with a sister of the former at Enfield, where the children were brought up. In the retired neighbourhood of Chase Side they took a house, which has since been pulled down ; it possessed a large, old-fashioned garden, in which the children found great delight. It would be an error to trace in the imaginary portrait, called *The Child in the House*, a definite picture of the early surroundings of Walter Pater. The existence at Enfield is hardly touched upon there, with the sole exception of the " cry on the stair," announcing the death of Florian Deleal's father ; this, it appears, is a reminiscence of the decease, not of his father, but of his grandmother, which was so announced to the household at

Enfield. So far as *The Child in the House* depicts a veritable scene, it presents to us Fish Hall, near Hadlow, Kent, the residence of his godmother and cousin, Mrs. Walter H. May ; this mansion, part of which was very old, was the favourite holiday-haunt of the little Paters, and a place of mystery and romance to Walter.

If, however, *The Child in the House* must be accepted very guardedly as giving an impression of the physical surroundings of Walter Pater's childhood, much more of actual reminiscence has been put into *Emerald Uthwart* (a story now reprinted in the *Miscellaneous Studies*). The first elements of education were given at the private house of the head-master of the grammar-school at Enfield, but the earliest crisis of Pater's life was the entrance into King's School, Canterbury, at the age of fourteen. The " old ecclesiastical city," to which Emerald proceeds, is Canterbury, closely and exactly described, and the features enumerated in the story—" the curiosities of the Precincts, the ' dark entry,' the rich heraldries of the blackened and mouldering cloister, the ruined overgrown spaces where the old monastery stood, the stones of which furnished material for the rambling prebends' houses "—these were features at Canterbury which immediately impressed the imagination of the shy and sensitive little boy, and remained with him through life as having given him his earliest experience of æsthetic pleasure.

It seems probable that, on the whole, this part of *Emerald Uthwart* may be taken as strictly autobiographical. Pater was happy at King's School, in spite of his complete indifference to outdoor games. In his first years at public school he was very idle and backward, nor was it till he reached the sixth form that his faculties seemed really to awaken. He is remembered as rather a popular boy, and as years went on his unquestioned ability inspired respect. On the day of Pater's funeral the Warden of Keble preached in the Cathedral of Canterbury, and was able to record, in touching phrases, the pride which the school had always felt in him, and Pater's own persistent attachment to the school. From the first, and before he went to Canterbury, Walter had been considered the " clever " one of the family ; not specially precocious, he was always meditative and serious—marked from the very first for the intellectual life. It is interesting to note that, quite without prompting from without, and while still at Enfield, all his thoughts were turned towards the Church. He loved best to organise a sort of solemn processional game, in which he took the part of bishop or cardinal. From the time when he first began to think of a future condition, his design was to be a clergyman ; never, curiously enough, a priest in the religion of his fathers, but in the Anglican ritual. Throughout life, it may here be said, even in his later days, when his thoughts turned back more and more to theological pre-occupations, Walter Pater never had any serious leaning towards Rome. Yet there can be little question that the heritage of his an-

cestors, in their obstinate adhesion to Catholicism,
had much to do with his haunting sense of the
value of the sensuous emblem, the pomp of colour
and melody, in the offices of religion. These
tendencies had received a great impetus while he
was yet a little boy, and had not proceeded to
Canterbury, from a visit he paid to a young friend
who lived at Hursley. Here he attracted the
attention of Keble, who walked and talked much
with him, and encouraged him in his religious
aspirations. Pater retained through life a vivid
recollection of this saintly man, although he never
saw him again.

Shortly before he left school, as he was entering
his twentieth year, Pater read *Modern Painters*,
and came very abruptly under the influence of
Ruskin. The world of art was now for the first
time opened to him. It is necessary at this point
to refute an extraordinary fable, widely circulated
at the time of his death, to the effect that the
finished and beautiful essay on " Winckelmann "
was written, and even printed, while the author
was a schoolboy at Canterbury. The idea is preposterous ; it was not until many years later that
Pater became aware of the existence of the German
critic, and his essay was composed and published
long after he was a Fellow of Brasenose. It is
singular, indeed, that he is not known to have made
any attempt to write, either as a schoolboy or an
undergraduate, his earliest essays being as mature
in style as the author was mature in years. Pater
made no painful experiments in authorship, or,

33

if he did, he kept them to himself. He did not begin to practise the art of writing until he had mastered all its secrets.

On June 11, 1858, he entered Queen's College, Oxford, as a commoner, with an exhibition from Canterbury ; and four years later, in the Michaelmas Term of 1862, he took his degree, gaining only a second class in *Literæ Humaniores*. Of these years of his undergraduate life it does not appear that there is much to reveal. In bare rooms, in the dim back quadrangle of his College, Pater worked quietly and unobtrusively, making few friends, very shy and silent, hardly observed in the noisy Oxford life of thirty-five years ago. He was the pupil of Mr. W. W. Capes, now rector of Liphook, then bursar and tutor of Queen's, and amongst those very rare spirits who divined the man he was to be was his earliest friend, Mr. Ingram Bywater, now Regius Professor of Greek. It is not understood that during these undergraduate days Pater's mind, a seed slowly germinating in the darkness, showed much partiality for pure literature or for plastic art. He was fascinated mainly by the study of logic and metaphysic, which were his pastimes, while the laborious business of classical scholarship occupied all but his leisure moments. Whether any record of these silent years remains, even with the few friends who shared them, seems doubtful. Pater never kept a diary, rarely wrote letters, and at this time offered no salient points for observation to seize upon. Yet one far - seeing man had noted the peculiar originality of Pater's temperament. Having in the ordinary course of his studies submitted some work to Jowett, that astute observer was so much struck with his power that he very generously offered to coach him for nothing. The offer was gratefully accepted, and Pater used to describe the thrill of gratification, and, still more, of astonishment, which he experienced when Jowett said to him one day, as he was taking his leave : " I think you have a mind that will come to great eminence." Unhappily, some years after there was a complete estrangement of sympathy between Jowett and Pater. But it is pleasant to record that, in the last year of the life of each, it was removed, and that Jowett was among those who congratulated Pater most cordially on his *Plato and Platonism*.

In 1862—his degree had been a disappointment —Pater, now three-and-twenty, took rooms in the High Street, Oxford, and read with private pupils. Of these Mr. T. H. S. Escott has told us in his pleasant reminiscences of Oxford that he was one. Another pupil, of somewhat later date, was Mr. Charles Lancelot Shadwell, now Fellow of Oriel, destined to become the most intimate of all Pater's friends, and now the guardian and editor of his papers. But still no definite aim seemed to have revealed itself to the future critic ; he was reading and meditating deeply, but he had as yet no call to create. Time went by ; in 1864 Pater was elected a Fellow of Brasenose College, and went into residence there. With this change in his material existence, a change came over his mind.

His sympathies grew wider and more human, he became more of a student of poetry, he formed more friendships, and was more assiduous in their cultivation. Of his earliest efforts after literary expression, all, it is believed, were destroyed by himself, with the solitary exception of the little study of a pure and brilliant spirit of youth, called "Diaphaneitè," of which the MS., dated July 1864, was found after his death and published by Mr. Shadwell in the *Miscellaneous Studies* of 1895. At last, in 1866, at the age of twenty-seven, he ventured to write and to print a little essay, a note or fragment, on Coleridge. We may read this first expression of a new writer to-day in the *Appreciations*. We shall find little of the peculiar charm of the mature Pater. His interest is solely in Coleridge, the metaphysician, the critic of thought ; that this same philosopher was an exquisite poet has not occurred to him, he positively forgets to mention the fact. As far as style is concerned, the little essay is correct and cold, without oddity, but with little trace of the harmonious felicity which was about to develop.

Vast is the change when we meet Walter Pater next. He had come from school with a tendency to value all things German. The teaching of Jowett and of T. H. Green tended to strengthen this habit, but Mr. Capes warned him against its excess, and endeavoured, at first with but little success, to attract him to the lucidity and gaiety of French literature. Pater's studies in philosophy now naturally brought him to Goethe, so massive an influence in the Oxford of that day, and the teaching of Goethe laid a deep impress upon his temperament, upon his whole outlook on the intellectual life. It was natural that one so delicately sensitive to the external symbol as was Pater should be prepared by the companionship of Goethe for the influence of a man who was Goethe's master in this one direction, and it was to a spirit inflammable in the highest degree that in 1866 was laid the torch of Otto Jahn's Life of Winckelmann, the *Biographische Aufsätze*. There was everything in the character and career of the great German restorer of Hellenic feeling to fascinate Pater, who seemed, through Ruskin, Goethe, and Hegel, to have travelled to his true prototype, to the one personality among the dead which was completely in sympathy with his own. Pater, too, among the sandhills of a spiritual Brandenburg, had held out arms of longing towards ideal beauty, revealed in physical or sensuous forms, yet inspired and interpenetrated with harmonious thought. The troubled feverish vision, the variegated and indeed over-decorated æsthetic of Ruskin, had become wearisome to Pater — not simple enough nor sensuous enough. Winckelmann was the master he wanted, who could " finger those pagan marbles with unsinged hands, with no sense of shame or loss," who could live serenely " in a world of exquisite but abstract and colourless form " ; and it was with the study of Winckelmann that he became himself a writer.

His famous essay on " Winckelmann " was the result of this new enthusiasm. It was published in the *Westminster Review* for January 1867, the author being now in his twenty-eighth year. From this time Pater's advance, though slow, was unbroken. Mr. John Morley having, in 1867, taken the editorship of the *Fortnightly Review*, called around him immediately a group of the most brilliant young men of the day. Walter Pater was in no undue haste to respond to the appeal. In 1868, inventing a name which has since sunken into disrepute and even ridicule, he wrote an essay on " Æsthetic Poetry," in which the early work of Mr. William Morris received prompt and judicious analysis. Then followed the series which are still so potent in their peculiar charm, the magnificent and most characteristic " Notes on Lionardo de Vinci," in November 1869 ; the " Fragment on Sandro Botticelli " in August 1870 ; the " Pico della Mirandula " in October, and the " Michelangelo " in November 1871. In 1873 most of these, and others, were published together in the memorable volume originally en titled *Studies in the History of the Renaissance*.

At this point he became partly famous. We may look back over the years which followed his fellowship, and see that, with the accession of humanistic ideas, he had gradually lost all belief in the Christian religion. This was the point, in his whole career, at which he was furthest from the Anglican faith. His intention, on relinquishing the idea of entering the Church of England, had been to become a Unitarian minister. This also he had abandoned by 1864. But that Pater's interest in ecclesiastical matters was never really dead, and that it soon began to revive, is proved by an anecdote with which the Bishop of Peterborough obliges me. He remembers dining with him in 1873, in company with Bonamy Price. Conversation turned on ecclesiastical matters, and Pater passed on to a dreamy monologue about the beauty of the Reserved Sacrament in Roman churches, which " gave them all the sentiment of a house where lay a dead friend." This immediately aroused the Protestantism of Bonamy Price, and a theological discussion ensued which waxed so warm that Dr. Creighton had to suggest a retreat to the drawing-room. When he came up for election at Brasenose it was as a non-clerical fellow—I think the first who ever was appointed there—that Pater took his place in the society. In the next year, in company with Mr. Shadwell, he paid his first visit to Italy, and at Ravenna, Pisa, Florence, formed those impressions of the art of the Renaissance which were so powerfully to colour all his own future work as an artist. In 1858, when he came to Oxford, his sisters had migrated to Heidelberg, and here it was his custom to spend the long vacation, making no friends among the Germans, however, and never, in all those years, troubling himself to learn to speak their language.

II

The costume of Walter Pater had been the ordinary academic dress of the don of the period, but in May 1869 he flashed forth at the Private View of the Royal Academy in a new top hat and a silk tie of brilliant apple - green. This little transformation marked a crisis ; he was henceforth no longer a provincial philosopher, but a critic linked to London and the modern arts. Where he touched the latter was through the Preraphaelites, especially through the extreme admiration he had conceived for the works of Mr. Burne - Jones, then much talked about, but rarely seen. At no time, I think, had he much personal knowledge either of that painter or of Rossetti. With Mr. Swinburne he became about that date more intimate. The poet was a not unfrequent visitor in those years to Pater's college rooms. To all young Oxford, then, the name of Mr. Swinburne was an enchantment, and there used to be envious traditions of an upper window in Brasenose Lane thrown open to the summer night, and, welling forth from it, a music of verse which first outsang and then silenced the nightingales, protracting its harmonies until it disconcerted the lark himself at sunrise.

After this, it is a notable instance of the art of sinking to record that I first set eyes on Pater in 1871, as he and Mr. Swinburne were dismounting from a hansom cab at Gabriel Rossetti's door in Cheyne Walk. Almost unknown to the world, he was already an object of respect to me as the author of those " Notes on Lionardo," which had seemed to give a new aspect to the whole conception of Italian art. In 1872 I was presented to him in the studio of William Bell Scott : it was not until the early months of 1874 that I first began to visit him at Oxford, and so opened a friendship which was never clouded for a moment in the course of more than twenty years. From this point, then, although my opportunities of seeing Pater, especially in Oxford, were but occasional, I can record something from personal knowledge.

In 1869, removing from Brasenose many of the pretty objects and *bric-à-brac* with which he had been the first man in Oxford to decorate college rooms, Pater furnished a little house in Norham Gardens, No. 2 Bradmore Road, his sisters returning from Heidelberg to keep house for him. Once settled here, Pater blossomed out into considerable sociability, entertaining and being entertained in the cordial Oxford way. He had now a large circle of pleasant acquaintances ; I cannot remember that he had many intimate friends. Besides those whom I have mentioned already, I can but recall Mark Pattison, Dr. Mandell Creighton (now Bishop of Peterborough), and Miss Mary Arnold, soon to marry an accomplished young member of Pater's own college, Mr. Humphry Ward. To these he would doubtless talk, to each in a different way, of the interests most deeply rooted in his heart, " of charm, and lucid order, and labour of the file," and to a very few London friends also. The rest of the world found him affable and acquiescent, already in those remote days displaying a little of that Renan manner which later on became emphasised, a manner which trifled gracefully and somewhat mysteriously with a companion not entirely in sympathy.

Pater's relation to the Rector of Lincoln was amusing. It was at once confiding and suspicious. "Pattison is charming," he used to murmur, "when he's good. Shall we go over and see if he is good this afternoon?" But he was worried by a certain wilfulness in the Rector; he could prove to be so far from good, so absolutely naughty. I remember on one occasion—I think in the autumn of 1875—when the Rector, on a visit at Bradmore Road, had been delicious: he had talked, in his most distinguished way, on a dozen rare and exquisite topics. He left, begging Pater to come to him next day, and kindly extending the invitation to me. Accordingly we went, but the charm was broken. A frivolous demon had entered into the Rector; he talked of croquet and of petticoats. We went back, sad and silent, to Bradmore Road, and, just as we reached home, Pater said, with solemn firmness, "What Pattison likes best in the world, no doubt, is romping with great girls in the gooseberry-bushes!"

The vacations in these years were very pleasant to Pater; they were almost always spent abroad —in France, in the company of his sisters. He would walk as much as possible, scouring a

42

neighbourhood for architectural features, and preserving those impressions of travel, which most of us lament to find so fugitive, with astonishing exactitude. He was no linguist, and French was the only language in which he could even make his wants understood. Although so much in Germany in his youth, he could speak no German. When he was travelling he always left a place, if anyone staying in the hotel spoke to him. He had no wish to be competent in modern languages ; he used to say : " Between you and me and the post, I hate a foreigner," and when exotic persons of distinction threatened to visit Brasenose, Pater used to disappear until he was sure that they had gone. He loved the North of France extremely, and knew it well. He was always planning a series of studies on the great ecclesiastical towns of France, yet wrote no more than a couple of these—on Amiens and on Vézelay. So eagerly did he prosecute these holiday tours, that he habitually over-walked himself, thus losing much of the benefit which he might otherwise have gained from the only form of exercise he ever indulged in. I note, in a letter of 1877, describing a visit to Azay-le-Rideau, this characteristic sentence: " We find always great pleasure in adding to our experiences of these French places, and return always a little tired indeed, but with our minds pleasantly full of memories of stained glass, old tapestries, and new wild flowers." These excursions rarely extended farther than the centre of France, but once, I think in 1882, Pater went alone to Rome, and spent the winter vacation there. He could ill endure exciting travel, or too rapid hurrying from one impressive place to another. His eye absorbed so slowly, and his memory retained what he saw so completely, that to be shown too much was almost physical pain to him, and yet he was always inflicting it upon himself.

Some time after I knew him first, that entertaining skit, *The New Republic,* was produced, and achieved great popular success. Pater had his niche in this gallery of caricatures, under the title of Mr. Rose. It has been represented that he suffered violent distress from this parody of his style and manner, that it caused him to retire from society and to abandon the prosecution of literature. Nothing in the world could be further from the truth. He thought the portrait a little unscrupulous, and he was discomposed by the freedom of some of its details. But he admired the cleverness and promise of the book, and it did not cause him to alter his mode of life or thought in the smallest degree. He was even flattered, for he was an author much younger and more obscure than most of those who were satirised, and he was sensible that to be thus distinguished was a compliment. What he liked less, what did really ruffle him, was the persistence with which the newspapers at this time began to attribute to him all sorts of " æsthetic " follies and extravagances. He said to me, in 1876 : " I wish they wouldn't call me ' a hedonist ' ; it produces such a bad effect

on the minds of the people who don't know Greek."
And the direct result of all these journalistic
mosquito-bites was the suppression of the famous
" Conclusion " in the second (1877) edition of his
Renaissance.

The source of his very long silence—for twelve
years divided his second book from his first—I
hardly know, unless it be attributed to the painful
slowness of his methods of composition, and his
extreme solicitude for perfection of style. At last,
in February 1885 was published his romance of
Marius the Epicurean, the work by which, I
believe, Pater will pre-eminently be known to
posterity. In the meantime had appeared, in the
Fortnightly Review, for 1876, several of those
Greek studies, on Demeter and Persephone, on
the Marbles of Ægina and the like, which Mr.
Shadwell collected in a posthumous volume in
1895 ; *The Child in the House*, too, in its earliest
form, belongs to 1878, though first published as
a book in the summer of 1894. The success of
Marius was as great as that of a book so grave and
strenuous could be. In 1887 Pater followed it by
a series of four *Imaginary Portraits*, studies in
philosophic fiction, one of which, " Denys l'Auxer-
rois," displays the peculiarities of his style with
more concentrated splendour than any other of
his writings. In 1889 he collected some of his
miscellaneous critical studies into a volume called
Appreciations, with an Essay on Style. In 1893
he published his highly finished college lectures on
Plato and Platonism in a volume of rare dignity

and humanistic beauty. Finally, in the early summer of 1894, *The Child in the House* was issued from the Oxford Press of Mr. Daniel, as a precious toy for bibliomaniacs. This list of publications practically resumes the events in Pater's life through twenty years.

During that period the household was moved once, in 1886, to Kensington, and again, in 1893, back to Oxford, where he fitted up a house in St. Giles. But, all the while, Pater's real home was in his rooms at Brasenose, where he passed a quiet, cloistered, and laborious existence, divided between his college duties and his books. His later years were comforted by a great deal of consideration and affection from those around him ; noiseless, as he was, and in a sense unexhilarating, he became increasingly an object of respectful admiration to young Oxford men, whom, on his part, he treated with the most courteous indulgence. Of this generation, one disciple came to proffer a tribute of hero-worship, and remained to become an intimate friend ; this was the Rev. F. W. Bussell, now Fellow of Brasenose, whose tender solicitude did much to render the latest of Pater's years agreeable to him. Pater acted for some time as dean and tutor of his college, entering assiduously into the councils and discipline of the society, but he never accepted, if indeed it were ever offered, any university office. He shrank from all multiplication of responsibility, from anything which should break in upon the sequestered and austere simplicity of his life. As time went on, a great change came over his relation to religious matters. When I had known him first he was a pagan, without any guide but that of the personal conscience ; years brought gradually with them a greater and greater longing for the supporting solace of a creed. His talk, his habits, became more and more theological, and it is my private conviction that, had he lived a few years longer, he would have endeavoured to take orders and a small college living in the country.

Report, which found so much to misrepresent in a life so orderly and simple, has erred even as to the place and occasion of his death. He was taken ill with rheumatic fever in the month of June 1894, being, as he remained to the end, not in college, but with his sisters in their house in St. Giles. He was recovering, and was well enough to be busy upon a study on *Pascal*, which he has left nearly completed, when, in consequence of writing too close to an open window, pleurisy set in and greatly reduced his strength. Again he seemed convalescent, and had left his room, without ill-effect, on July 29, when, repeating the experiment next day, the action of the heart failed, and he died, on the staircase of his house, in the arms of his sister, at ten o'clock on the morning of Monday, July 30, 1894. Had he lived five days longer, he would have completed his fifty-fifth year. He was buried, in the presence of many of his oldest friends, in the beautiful cemetery of St. Giles at Oxford.

III

When Pater was first seized with an ambition to write, the individuals of his own age with whom he came into competition were mainly poets. Those were the early days of Gabriel and Christina Rossetti, of Morris, of Swinburne ; and most of the still younger men made their first steps in the field of verse, however far they might afterwards diverge from it. Pater, in this nest of singing-birds, resolved to be in prose no less painstaking, no less elaborate, no less bound by rule and art than the poets were. He is to be distinguished from those who had so much to say that their speech was forced out of them in a torrent, nor less from those whose instinct led them to bubble forth in periods of a natural artless grace. If we take these symbols of a mountain-stream or of a fountain for other prose-writers who have won the ear of the public with little effort, then for Pater the appropriate image seems the artesian well, to reach the contents of which, strata of impermeable clay must be laboriously bored. It was not that there was any lack of material there, nor any doubt about the form it must take when it emerged, but that it was so miraculously deep down and hard to reach. I have known writers of every degree, but never one to whom the act of composition was such a travail and an agony as it was to Pater.

In his earlier years the labour of lifting the sentences was so terrific that anyone with less fortitude would have entirely abandoned the effort.

I recollect the writing of the opening chapters of
Marius, and the stress that attended it—the in-
tolerable languor and fatigue, the fevers and the
cold fits, the grey hours of lassitude and insomnia,
the toil as at a deep petroleum well when the oil
refuses to flow. With practice, this terrific effort
grew less. A year or two ago I was reminding
him of those old times of storm and stress, and
he replied, " Ah ! it is much easier now. If I live
long enough, no doubt I shall learn quite to like
writing." The public saw the result of the labour
in the smooth solidity of the result, and could
suppose, from the very elaboration, that great
pains had been taken. How much pains, very few
indeed can have guessed !

It may be of interest to record the manner in
which this most self-conscious and artistic of prose-
writers proceeded. First of all, another pretty
fable must be knocked on the head. It has been
said, and repeated, that Pater composed his best
sentences without any relation to a context, and
wrote them down on little squares of paper, ready to
stick them in at appropriate and effective places.
This is nonsense ; it is quite true that he used such
squares of paper, but it was for a very different
purpose. He read with a box of these squares
beside him, jotting down on each, very roughly,
anything in his author which struck his fancy,
either giving an entire quotation, or indicating a
reference, or noting a disposition. He did not
begin, I think, any serious critical work without
surrounding himself by dozens of these little loose

notes. When they were not direct references or citations, they were of the nature of a *memoria technica*. Here is an example :

" Something about the gloomy Byzantine archit., belfries, solemn night come in about the birds attracted by the Towers."

Here is another :

" ? did he suppose predestination to have taken place, only *after* the Fall ? "

These papers would be placed about him, like the pieces of a puzzle, and when the right moment came the proper square would serve as a monitor or as a guide.

Having prepared his box of little squares, he would begin the labour of actual composition, and so conscious was he of the modifications and additions which would supervene that he always wrote on ruled paper, leaving each alternate line blank. Mr. Austin Dobson reminds me that Goldsmith did the same. On this broad canvas of alternate lines, then, Pater would slowly begin to draw his composition, the cartoon of what would in time be a finished essay. In the first draft the phrase would be a bald one ; in the blank alternate line he would at leisure insert fresh descriptive or parenthetical clauses, other adjectives, more exquisitely related adverbs, until the space was filled. It might then be supposed that the MS. was complete. Far from it ! Cancelling sheet by sheet, Pater then began to copy out the whole—as before, on alternate lines of copy-book pages ; this revise was treated in the same way—

corrected, enlarged, interleaved, as it were, with minuter shades of feeling and more elaborate apparatus of parenthesis.

No wonder that certain disadvantages were attendant upon the excessive finish of such a style. It is not possible to work in this way, with a cold hammer, and yet to avoid a certain deadness and slipperiness of surface. Pater's periods, in attaining their long-drawn harmony and fullness, were apt to lose vigour. Their polish did not quite make up for their languor, for the faintness and softness which attended their slow manipulation. Verse will bear an almost endless labour of the file ; prose, as the freer and more spontaneous form, is less happy in subjection to it. " What long sentences Plato writes ! " Pater says in his *Platonism*, and no doubt Plato might return the compliment. The sentences of the Oxford critic are often too long, and they are sometimes broken-backed with having had to bear too heavy a burden of allusion and illustration. His style, however, was his peculiarity. It had beautiful qualities, if we have to confess that it had the faults of those qualities. It was highly individual ; it cannot be said that he owed it to any other writer, or that at any period of his thirty years of literary labour he faltered or swerved from his own path. He was to a high degree self-centred. Pater did not study his contemporaries ; a year or two ago, he told me that he had read scarcely a chapter of Mr. Stevenson and not a line of Mr. Kipling. " I feel, from what I hear about them," he said, " that they are strong ; they might lead me out of my path. I want to go on writing in my own way, good or bad. I should be afraid to read Kipling, lest he should come between me and my page next time I sat down to write." It was the excess of a very native and genuine modesty. He, too, was strong, had he but known it, strong enough to have resisted the magnets of contemporary style. Perhaps his own writing might have grown a little simpler and a little more supple if he had had the fortitude to come down and fight among his fellows.

IV

Walter Pater was another of those discreet spirits who, like Gray, " never speak out." He was cautious, reserved, and shy in his relations even with his friends ; he seemed to possess no medium through which to approach them very closely. An extremely affectionate disposition took the place of expansiveness, and the young people who in later years gathered around him mistook the one for the other. Each found in Pater what he brought ; each saw in that patient, courteous, indulgent mirror a pleasant reflection of himself. The inaccessibility of Pater is another of those fables which have to be destroyed ; no one was less a hermit, no one was more easily amused or better pleased to bid a congenial companion welcome. He was an assiduous host, a gracious listener ; but who could tell what was passing behind those half-shut, dark-grey eyes, that courteous and gentle mask ? He liked the human race, one is inclined to say, liked its noise and neighbourhood, if it were neither too loud nor too near, but his faith in it was never positive, nor would he trust it to read his secret thoughts.

I have already suggested his likeness to Renan in the attitude of his mind. The great Frenchman has described, in his autobiography, the tendency which led him to refrain from opposition and argument, and to bow the head in the conversational house of Rimmon. Walter Pater had these concessions, mere escapes of the soul from undue pressure, and he had, too, quite unconsciously, some of the very tricks of speech of Renan —especially the " no doubt " that answered to the Frenchman's incessant " n'en doutez pas." With natures like his, in which the tide of physical spirits runs low, in which the vitality is lukewarm, the first idea in the presence of anything too vivacious is retreat, and the most obvious form of social retreat is what we call " affectation." It is not to be denied that, in the old days, Pater, startled by strangers, was apt to seem affected : he retreated as into a fortress, and enclosed himself in a sort of solemn effeminacy. It was, at its worst, mild in comparison with what the masters of preposterous behaviour have since accustomed us to, but it reminded one too much of Mr. Rose. It was put on entirely for the benefit of strangers, and to his inner circle of friends it seemed like a joke. Perhaps in some measure it was a joke ; no one could ever quite tell whether Pater's strange *rictus* was closer to laughter or to tears.

A nature so enclosed as his, so little capable of opening its doors to others, must have some outlet of relief. Pater found his outlet in a sort of delicate, secret playfulness. There are animals which sit all day immovable and humped up among the riot of their fellows, and which, when all the rest of the menagerie is asleep, steal out upon their slip of greensward and play the wildest pranks in the light of the moon. Pater has often reminded me of some such armadillo or wombat. That childishness which is the sign - manual of genius used to come out in the oddest way when he was perfectly at home. Those who think of him as a solemn pundit of æsthetics may be amazed to know that he delighted in very simple and farcical spectacles and in the broadest of humour. His favourite among modern playwrights was Mr. Pinero, and I shall never forget going with him to see *The Magistrate*, when that piece was originally produced. Not a schoolboy in the house was more convulsed with laughter, more enchanted at the romping " business " of the play, than the author of *Marius*. He had the gift, when I knew him first, of inventing little farcical dialogues, into which he introduced his contemporaries ; in these the Rector of Lincoln generally figured, and Pater had a rare art of imitating Pattison's speech and peevish intonation. One playful fancy, per- sisted in so long that even close and old friends were deceived by it, was the figment of a group of relations—Uncle Capsicum and Uncle Guava, Aunt Fancy (who fainted when the word " leg " was mentioned), and Aunt Tart (for whom no acceptable present could ever be found). These shadowy personages had been talked about for so many years that at last, I verily believe, Pater had almost persuaded himself of their existence. Perhaps these little touches will be thought too trifling to be mentioned, but I hold that they were all a part and parcel of his complex and shrouded intellectual life, and therefore not to be forgotten.

He had great sweetness and uniformity of temper, and almost the only thing that ever ruffled him was a reference to an act of vandalism committed at Brasenose while he was on the governing body. The college had a group, called " Cain and Abel," cast in lead, a genuine work by John of Bologna. For some reason or other this was thought inconvenient, and was sold for old lead, a somewhat barbarous proceeding. Pater, from indolence, or else from indifference to late Italian sculpture, did not stir a finger to prevent this desecration, and in later years a perfectly unfailing mode of rousing him would be to say, artlessly, " Was there not once a group by John of Bologna in the college ? " However sunken in reverie, however dreamily detached, Pater would sit up in a moment, and say, with great acidity, " It was totally devoid of merit, no doubt."

Pater showed much tact and good sense in his attitude towards the college life. He lectured rarely, I believe, in later years ; in the old days he was an assiduous tutor. His temperament, it is true, sometimes made it difficult to work with him. On one occasion, at the examination for scholarships, he undertook to look over the English essays ; when the examiners met to compare marks, Pater had none. He explained, with languor, " They did not much impress me." As something had to be done, he was asked to endeavour to recall such impressions as he had formed ; to stimulate his memory, the names were read out in alphabetical order. Pater shook his head mournfully as each was pronounced, murmuring dreamily, " I do not recall him," " He did not strike me," and so on. At last the reader came to the name of Sanctuary, on which Pater's face lit up, and he said, " Yes ; I remember ; I liked his name."

My friend, Dr. Henry Jackson, gives me an anecdote which illustrates a more practical side to his character. In 1870, having just begun to lecture at Trinity, our Cambridge Platonist found himself seated next Pater at dinner in Brasenose. He said to him : " I believe you lecture constantly on *The Republic*. How do you get through it in time ? It seems as though lecturing three times a week for three terms, it would be impossible to deal adequately within a year with all the problems and the fallacies." " Oh ! " said Pater, " I always, begin by telling them that Socrates is not such a fool as he seems, and we get through nicely in two terms." He grew more and more inclined to take an indulgent view of the young people.

A year or two ago, I remember his saying, when somebody asked him whether the horse-play of the undergraduates did not disturb him, " Oh ! no ; I rather enjoy it. They are like playful young tigers, that have been fed." He was not a " progressive " ; our friend the Bishop of Peterborough recalls a serious discussion in commonroom at Brasenose, on the burning subject of university reform. Pater interposed in the thick of the fray with the somewhat disconcerting remark, " I do not know what your object is. At present the undergraduate is a child of nature ; he grows up like a wild rose in a country lane ; you want to turn him into a turnip, rob him of all grace, and plant him out in rows." And his remark, concerning bonfires in the quad, that they lighted up the spire of St. Mary's so beautifully, will long be remembered.

The perennial conflict in his members, between his exquisite instinct for corporeal beauty on the one hand and his tendency to ecclesiastical symbol and theological dogma on the other, is the secret, I think, of what made the character of Pater so difficult for others to elucidate, in some measure also so painful and confusing for himself. He was not all for Apollo, nor all for Christ, but each deity swayed in him, and neither had that perfect homage that brings peace behind it. As Alphonse Daudet says of some thinker, " Son cerveau était une cathédrale désaffectée," and when he tried, as he bade us try, " to burn always with the hard, gem-like flame " of æsthetic observation, the flame of another altar mingled with the fire and darkened it. Not easily or surely shall we divine the workings of a brain and a conscience scarcely less complex, less fantastic, less enigmatical, than the face of Mona Lisa herself. Pater, as a human being, illustrated by no letters, by no diaries, by no impulsive unburdenings of himself to associates, will grow more and more shadowy. But it has seemed well to preserve, while still they are attainable, some of the external facts about a writer whose polished and concentrated work has already become part of the classic literature of England, and who will be remembered among the writers of this age when all but a few are forgotten.

September 1894.

THE CHARM OF STERNE

THE CHARM OF STERNE [1]

IT is exactly two hundred years to-night since there was born, at Clonmel, in Ireland, a son to a subaltern in an English regiment just home from the Low Countries. " My birthday," Laurence Sterne tells us, " was ominous to my poor father, who was, the day after our arrival, with many other brave officers, broke and sent adrift into the wide world with a wife and two children." The life of the new baby was one of perpetual hurry and scurry ; his mother, who had been an old campaigner, daughter of what her son calls " a noted suttler " called Nuttle, had been the widow of a soldier before she married Roger Sterne. In the extraordinary fashion of the army of those days, the regiment was hurried from place to place—as was that of the father of the infant Borrow a century later—and with it hastened the unhappy Mrs. Sterne, for ever bearing and for ever losing children, " most rueful journeys," marked by a long succession of little tombstones left behind. Finally, at Gibraltar, the weary father, pugnacious to the last, picked a quarrel about a goose and was pinked through the body, surviving in a thoroughly damaged condition, to die, poor exhausted pilgrim of Bellona, in barracks in Jamaica.

[1] Address delivered to the Authors' Club, November 24, 1913.

It would be difficult to imagine a childhood better calculated than this to encourage pathos in a humorist and fun in a sentimentalist. His account, in his brief autobiography, of the appearance and disappearance of his hapless brothers and sisters is a proof of how early life appealed to Laurence Sterne in the dappled colours of an April day. We read there of how at Wicklow, " we lost poor Joram, a pretty boy " ; how " Anne, that pretty blossom, fell in the barracks of Dublin " ; how little Devijehar was " left behind " in Carrickfergus. We know not whether to sob or to giggle, so tragic is the rapid catalogue of dying babies, so ridiculous are their names and fates. Here, then, I think, we have revealed to us the prime characteristic of Sterne, from which all his other characteristics branch away, for evil or for good. As no other writer since Shakespeare, and in a different and perhaps more intimate way than even Shakespeare, he possessed the key of those tears that succeed the hysteria of laughter, and of that laughter which succeeds the passion of tears. From early childhood, and all through youth and manhood, he had been collecting observations upon human nature in these rapidly alternating moods.

He observed it in its frailty, but being exquisitely frail himself, he was no satirist. A breath of real satire would blow down the whole delicate fabric of *Tristram Shandy* and *The Sentimental Journey*. Sterne pokes fun at people and things ; he banters the extravagance of private humour ; but it is always with a consciousness that he is himself more extravagant than anyone. If we compare him for a moment with Richardson, who buttonholes the reader in a sermon ; or with Smollett, who snarls and bites like an angry beast ; we feel at once that Sterne could not breathe in the stuffiness of the one or in the tempest of the other. Sympathy is the breath of his nostrils, and he cannot exist except in a tender, merry relation with his readers. His own ideal, surely, is that which he attributed to the fantastic and gentle Yorick, who never could enter a village, but he caught the attention of old and young. " Labour stood still as he passed ; the bucket hung suspended in the middle of the well ; the spinning - wheel forgot its round, even chuck-farthing and shuffle-cap themselves stood gaping till he had got out of sight." Like Yorick, Sterne loved a jest in his heart.

There are, it seems to me, two distinct strains in the intellectual development of Sterne, and I should like to dwell upon them for a moment, because I think a lack of recognition of them has been apt to darken critical counsel in the consideration of his writings. You will remember that he was forty-six years of age before he took up the business of literature seriously. Until that time he had been a country parson in Yorkshire, carrying his body, that "cadaverous bale of goods," from Sutton to Stillington, and from Stillington to Skelton. He had spent his life in riding, shooting, preaching, joking, and philandering in company, and after a fashion, most truly reprehensible from a clerical point of view, yet admirably fitted to prepare such an artist for his destined labours as a painter of the oddities of average Englishmen. But by the side of this indolent search after the enjoyment of the hour, Sterne cultivated a formidable species of literature in which he had so few competitors that in after years, his indolence prompted him to plagiarise freely from sources which, surely, no human being would discover. He steeped himself in the cumbrous learning of those writers of the Renaissance in whom congested Latin is found tottering into colloquial French. He studied Rabelais perhaps more deeply than any other Englishman of his time and certainly Beroalde de Verville, Bruscambille, and other absurdities of the sixteenth century were familiar to him and to him alone in England.

Hence, when Sterne began to write, there were two streams flowing in his brain, and these were, like everything else about him, inconsistent with one another. The faithful tender colour of modern life competed with the preposterous oddity of burlesque erudition. When he started the annals of Tristram Shandy, the Rabelais vein was in the ascendant, and there is plenty of evidence that it vastly dazzled and entertained readers of that day. But it no longer entertains us very much, and it is the source of considerable injustice done by modern criticism to the real merits of Sterne. When so acute a writer as Bagehot condemns much of *Tristram Shandy* as " a sort of antediluvian fun, in which uncouth saurian jokes play idly in an unintelligible world," he hits the nail on the head of why so many readers nowadays turn with impatience from that work. But they should persevere, for Sterne himself saw his error, and gradually dropped the " uncouth saurian jokes " which he had filched out of Burton and Beroalde, relying more and more exclusively on his own rich store of observations taken directly from human nature. In the adorable seventh volume of *Tristram*, and in *The Sentimental Journey*, there is nothing left of Rabelais except a certain rambling artifice of style.

The death of Sterne, at the age of fifty-four, is one of those events which must be continually regretted, because to the very end of his life he was growing in ease and ripeness, was discovering more perfect modes of self-expression, and was purging himself of his compromising intellectual frailties. It is true that from the very first his excellences were patent. The portrait of my Uncle Toby, which Hazlitt truly said is " one of the finest compliments ever paid to human nature," occurs, or rather begins, in the second volume of *Tristram Shandy*. But the marvellous portraits which the early sections of that work contain are to some extent obscured, or diluted, by the author's determination to gain piquancy by applying old methods to new subjects. Frankly, much as I love Sterne, I find Kunastrockius and Lithopaedus a bore. I suspect they have driven more than one modern reader away from the enjoyment of *Tristram Shandy*.

Towards the end of the eighteenth century a leading Dissenting minister, the Rev. Joseph Fawcett, said in answer to a question : " Do I *like* Sterne ? Yes, to be sure I should deserve to be hanged if I didn't ! " That was the attitude of thoughtful and scrupulous people of cultivation more than one hundred years ago. But it was their attitude only on some occasions. There is no record of the fact, but I am ready to believe that Mr. Fawcett may, with equal sincerity, have said that Sterne was a godless wretch. We know that Bishop Warburton presented him with a purse of gold, in rapturous appreciation of his talents, and then in a different mood described him as " an irrevocable scoundrel." No one else has ever flourished in literature who has combined such alternating powers of attraction and repulsion. We like Sterne extremely at one moment, and we dislike him no less violently at another. He is attar of roses to-day and asafœtida to-morrow, and it is not by any means easy to define the elements which draw us towards him and away from him. Like Yorick, he had " a wild way of talking," and he wrote impetuously and impudently " in the naked temper which a merry heart discovered." As he " seldom shunned occasions of saying what came uppermost, and without much ceremony, he had but too many temptations in life of scattering his wit and his humour, his gibes and his jests, about him."

So that even if he had been merely Yorick, Sterne would have had manifold opportunities of giving offence and causing scandal. But he was not only a humorist with " a thousand little sceptical notions to defend," but he was a sentimentalist as well. These two characteristics he was constantly mingling, or trying to mingle, since sentimentality and humour are in reality like oil and wine. He would exasperate his readers by throwing his wig in their faces at the moment when they were weeping, or put them out of countenance by ending a farcical story on a melancholy note. A great majority of Englishmen like to be quite sure of the tone of what they read ; they wish an author to be straightforward ; they dread irony and they loathe impishness. Now Sterne is the most impish of all imaginative writers. He is what our grandmothers, in describing the vagaries of the nursery, used to call " a limb of Satan." Tristram Shandy, in his light-hearted way, declared that " there's not so much difference between good and evil as the world is apt to imagine." No doubt that is so, but the world does not like its preachers to play fast and loose with moral definitions.

The famous sensibility of Sterne was a reaction against the seriousness, the ponderosity, of previous prose literature in England. We talk of the heaviness of the eighteenth century, but the periods of even such masters of solid rhetoric as Johnson and Gibbon are light as thistledown in comparison with the academic prose of the seventeenth century. Before the eighteenth century is called lumbering, let us set a page of Hume against a page of Hobbes, or a passage out of Berkeley by a passage out of Selden. Common justice is seldom done to the steady clarification of English prose between 1660 and 1750, but it was kept within formal lines until the sensitive recklessness of Sterne broke up the mould, and gave it the flying forms of a cloud or a wave. He owed this beautiful inspiration to what Nietzsche calls his " squirrel-soul," which leaped from bough to bough, and responded without a trace of conventional restraint to every gust of emotion. Well might Goethe be inspired to declare that Sterne was the most emancipated spirit of his century.

His very emancipation gives us the reason why Sterne's admirers nowadays are often divided in their allegiance to him. A frequent part of his humour deals very flippantly with subjects that are what we have been taught to consider indelicate or objectionable. It is worse than useless to try to explain this foible of his away, because he was aware of it and did it on purpose. He said that " nothing but the more gross and carnal parts of a composition will go down." His indecency was objected to in his own age, but not with any excluding severity. And I would like to call your attention to the curious conventionality of our views on this subject. Human nature does not change, but it changes its modes of expression. In the eighteenth century very grave people, even bishops, allowed themselves, in their relaxed moments, great licence in jesting. Yet they would have been scandalised by the tragic treatment of sex by our more audacious novelists of to-day. We are still interested in these matters, but we have agreed not to joke about them. I read the other day a dictum of one of those young gentlemen who act as our moral policemen : he prophesied that a jest on a sexual subject would, in twenty years, be not merely reprehensible, as it is now, but unintelligible. Very proper, no doubt, only do not let us call this morality, it is only a change of habits.

Sterne is not suited to readers who are disheartened at irrelevancy. It is part of his charm, and it is at the same time his most whimsical habit, never to proceed with his story when you expect him to do so, and to be reminded by his own divagations of delightful side - issues which lead you, entranced, whither you had no intention of going. He did not merely not shun occasions of being irrelevant, but he sought them out and eagerly cultivated them. Remember that a whole chapter of *Tristram* is devoted to the *attitude* of Corporal Trim as he prepared himself to read the Sermon. Sterne kept a stable of prancing, plump little hobby-horses, and he trotted them out upon every occasion. But this is what makes his books the best conversational writing in the English language. He writes for all the world exactly as though he were talking at his ease, and we listen enchanted to the careless, frolicking, idle, penetrating speaker who builds up for us so nonchalantly, with persistent but unobtrusive touch upon touch, the immortal figures of Mr. Shandy, my Uncle Toby, Trim, Yorick, the Widow Wadman, and so many more.

This, I am inclined to think, in drawing this brief sketch to an end, is Sterne's main interest for ourselves. He broke up the rhetorical manner of composition, or, rather, he produced an alternative manner which was gradually accepted and is in partial favour still. I would ask you to read for yourselves the scene of the ass who blocked the way for Tristram at Lyons, and to consider how completely new that method of describing, of facing a literary problem, was in 1765. I speak here to an audience of experts, to a company of authors who are accustomed to a close consideration of the workmanship of their *métier*. I ask them where, at all events in English, anything like that scene had been found before the days of Sterne. Since those days we have never been without it.

To trace the Shandean influence down English literature for the last century and a half would take me much too long for your patience. In Dickens, in Carlyle, even in Ruskin, the Shandean element is often present and not rarely predominant. None of those great men would have expressed himself exactly as he does but for Laurence Sterne. And coming down to our own time, I see the influence of Sterne everywhere. The pathos of Sir James Barrie is intimately related to that of the creator of Uncle Toby and Maria of Moulines, while I am not sure that of all the books which Stevenson read it was not *The Sentimental Journey* which made the deepest impression upon him.

WINE AND MR. SAINTSBURY

WINE AND MR. SAINTSBURY

LEIGH HUNT, who never possessed a cellar, but who would, had time permitted, have much appreciated dining with Mr. Saintsbury, conceived the appointment of an official " Jury of Tasters," who should be a board of elderly gentlemen " with the most thoughtful faces." He imagined them sitting in high appeal, profoundly ruminating on the pretensions of such a soufflé or such a vintage. Since his day the subject has received insufficient attention. Did the Grilled Red Mullet go with the Château Yqueam of 1870, or would a White Hermitage of 1865 have supplied a finer harmony ? This is the sort of question which such a board would have to decide, and of its importance no thinking man of any sensibility can entertain a doubt. There would have to be a chairman, and his election would be a matter of much serious discussion. In these days the round man is too often pushed into the square hole, but if justice and reason were combined in the choice, Mr. Saintsbury could not fail to be selected. If there be any person ignorant of the fact that he is the prince of living gourmets, his *Notes on a Cellar-Book* would be sufficient to silence the infidel. He had long enjoyed his œnological doctorate, and here at last is his thesis.

In these days, when an implacable intolerance has subdued one continent and threatened another, it requires some courage to defend the qualities and benefits of wine, not merely with no shadow of apology, but with the zeal of an apostle. Probably the gravest error in tactics which the advocates of a moderate use of alcohol have committed is that they have adopted an apologetic air. They have allowed themselves to be intimidated by the enemy, and have retired, instead of pushing the war into his country. The Pusillanimity of the Moderate Drinker would be a capital subject for an essay in a competitive examination. The creature really is too chicken-hearted. He allows the teetotal lecturer to assert that a single glass of light claret destroys the body and soul of man as devastatingly as an orgy on Siamese gin—a beverage which I once tasted and never shall forget. He is ashamed of what he should be proud of, namely, his liberty to gratify his own innocent tastes with no other guide but discretion and common sense.

Mr. Saintsbury will have none of such poltroonery. He tramples on the pride of Diogenes with a greater pride than his. He says, firmly, that " there is absolutely no scientific proof, of a trustworthy kind, that moderate consumption of sound alcoholic liquor does a healthy body any harm at all; while, on the other hand, there is the unbroken testimony of all history that alcoholic liquors have been used by the strongest, wisest, handsomest, and in every way best races of all times." His cheery book is written in this spirit throughout, and is remarkable for nothing more than for its magnificent refusal to be browbeaten by any Pussyfoot, whether American or native.

The language of gusto and rapture which Mr. Saintsbury employs, often quite lyrically, in his rich commendation of wine, may sometimes seem to be excessive, but a little exaggeration may surely be permitted to counterbalance the audacities of the professional prohibitionist. Perhaps the truth lies midway, as it often does. A very grave physician of authority, Dr. Thudichum, remarked in his *Cantor Lectures*, nearly half a century ago, that pure wine " rouses the higher faculties of thought, memory, and imagination, and increases the zest of life and its duration." Dr. Thudichum had met with a person who had undermined his health by an indiscriminate use of sherry, but we may advance that there is a great deal which was then and is still called *vino de pasta* which burns the inside far more than it comforts it. The learned doctor was quite aware of this, and warned his patients to be careful to drink nothing but " sound " wine, and that moderately, with due regard to individual habits and conditions. He wrote, however, entirely in the interests of truth, at a time when political passion and international intrigue had not burst open our cellars and emptied their contents. Wine is essentially the solace of early maturity ; as we advance in life, neither the palate nor the stomach can any longer be trusted, and it is possible that the decline in the popularity

of wine is a symbol that the round earth is sinking
into senility.

In his earliest chapters, Mr. Saintsbury is,
perhaps, a little too closely bound to his cellar-book.
He becomes more amusing when he feels free
to diverge into general considerations. With the
strongest exercise of the imagination, it is difficult
to share the raptures which a catalogue of ports
still gives to a man who was fortunate enough to
drink them thirty years ago. We read of " a
curious Dow " which was completely tawny in
character, of the wonderfully rapid development
of " the '04s," and (with regret) of a delicate
Ventozello of '72, which began to be " slightly
senescent " after 1902. We learn that Mr.
Saintsbury, in bygone years, found " more than
mere satisfaction in two outsiders—Gentiles, as it
were, or at least trans-Jordanians to the pure
Israel of Medoc—to wit, Pape Clément and Haut
Brion Larrivet." We receive these utterances
with respect, but we wish that Mr. Saintsbury
could restore something of the ecstasy :

> Could I revive within me
> The symphony and song,
> To such a deep delight 'twould win me
> That with music loud and long

I would ride out *cap-à-pie* to shiver a lance with
the teetotallers. But alas ! fancy cannot build
so well as to explain why, towards the close of last
century, Mr. Saintsbury derived less enjoyment
from a Richebourg of '69 than he did from a

Romanée Conti of '58. We can restore this distinction no more vividly than we can recapture the smack on the palate with which the Emperor Commodus must have read the list of the world's best wines which was drafted for him by the grammarian Pollux.

The wines of the ancients must have been very disagreeable. Pussyfoot is welcome to the famous Falernian which had the honey of Mount Hymettus mingled with it, and to those famous Sicilian vintages into which were grated aloes and tar, dried figs and myrrh. " Fill high the bowl with Samian wine " for Byron, if he likes, but not for me. I have no confidence in myrrh as an addition to a fruity port. However, Mr. Saintsbury does not touch on the antiquity of wines, nor on the heresy of the Spartans, who practised a prohibition of their own as a class-distinction, their slaves being urged to drink as a symbol of the contempt in which they were held, while the masters strictly confined themselves to soda-water or its archaic equivalent.

The Romans concocted a wine of turnips, which was sovereign against the fatigues of war. This might, with no small advantage, be introduced to-day for general use in Central Europe. I doubt whether it competed favourably with the rich libations of a Rhodian vintage, but these idle divagations are taking me too far from Mr. Saintsbury's cellar, which in its time has held treasures more pleasing than were known to the most luxurious of the ignorant heathen.

We have long been buoyed up with the hope that Mr. Saintsbury would write a History of Wine. He admits that he actually began such a work, and his reasons for abandoning it, which everybody must regret, are characteristic. He says :

" There would have been a considerable literature to look up ; and while I was not favourably situated in respect of access to it, my original farewell had been no trick, but the result of a genuine sense that I was getting too old for such a work. It would need infinite research to satisfy my own ideas of thoroughness ; for I have never yet given a second-hand opinion of any thing, or book, or person. Also, I should have had to drink more good wine than would now be good for my pocket, or perhaps even my health, and more bad than I could contemplate without dismay in my advancing years."

The last consideration, indeed, is one which will call forth a response from every delicate bosom, for it is a horrible thought that Mr. Saintsbury, who has taken so much pains throughout his honoured life to drink none but the finest liquor, might have filled his closing years with bitterness by imbibing quantities of bad wine in the service of historical thoroughness.

No one must miss Mr. Saintsbury's chapter on " Liqueurs," which is extremely diverting. Zola wrote a short story, called (I think) *La Fête à Coqueville*, describing how a ship laden with bénédictine and curaçao ran ashore on the rocks

of a Norman fishing village, and how uproariously
its cargo was appreciated by the inhabitants.
When the bacchanal was over, the silly fisher-
folk lay about upon the sands, and were sorry for
themselves. Mr. Saintsbury, so indulgent to real
wines, is rather harsh to liqueurs ; he thinks
several of them " a trifle sickly." But he remembers with thankfulness a curaçao which he
procured, between forty and fifty years ago, " at
the well-known house of Justerini and Brooks in
the vanished Opera Colonnade." Alas ! for the
trappestines of yester - year and the chartreuses
that are no more ! How old and sad we are
growing ! Yet Mr. Saintsbury still finds something attractive in " the straw envelope of a
maraschino bottle." O joy that in our embers
is *something* that doth live ! An anecdote of how
the late Bishop of London, Creighton, was believed
to have poisoned the landlord of his Oxford
lodgings with a glass of absinthe, is very pleasing

On beverages, which intrude rather im-
portunately upon a disquisition on wines, Mr.
Saintsbury is lively, but not so serious as might
be wished. He speaks with levity of cider, a
national drink of great merit, and of perry with
something like contempt. What Cowley calls
" the gentler apple's winy juice " is, he declares,
" not to be drunk without caution, and sometimes
has to be given up altogether from medical
aspects." This stigma on cider surprises me
from one who has drunk 1780 Madeira without
the smallest inconvenience.

CHRISTINA ROSSETTI

CHRISTINA ROSSETTI

WOMAN, for some reason which seems to have escaped the philosopher, has never taken a very prominent position in the history of poetry. But she has rarely been absent altogether from any great revival of poetic literature. The example of her total absence which immediately flies to the recollection is the most curious of all. That Shakespeare should have had no female rival, that the age in which music burdened every bough, and in which poets made their appearance in hundreds, should have produced not a solitary authentic poetess, even of the fifth rank, this is curious indeed. But it is as rare as curious, for though women have not often taken a very high position on Parnassus, they have seldom thus wholly absented themselves. Even in the iron age of Rome, where the Muse seemed to bring forth none but male children, we find, bound up with the savage verses of Juvenal and Persius, those seventy lines of pure and noble indignation against the brutality of Domitian which alone survive to testify to the genius of Sulpicia.

If that distinguished lady had come down to us in seventy thousand verses instead of seventy lines, would her fame have been greatly augmented ? Probably not. So far as we can observe, the strength of the great poet-women has been in their selection. Not a single poetess whose fame is old enough to base a theory upon has survived in copious and versatile numbers. Men like Dryden and Victor Hugo can strike every chord of the lyre, essay every mode and species of the art, and impress us by their bulk and volume. One very gifted and ambitious Englishwoman of the last generation, Elizabeth Barrett Browning, essayed to do the same. But her success, it must be admitted, grows every day more dubious. Where she strove to be passionate she was too often hysterical ; a sort of scream spoils the effect of all her full tirades. She remains readable mainly where she is exquisite, and one small volume would suffice to contain her probable bequest to posterity.

It is no new theory that women, in order to succeed in poetry, must be brief, personal, and concentrated. This was recognised by the Greek critics themselves. Into that delicious garland of the poets which was woven by Meleager to be hung outside the gate of the Gardens of the Hesperides he admits but two women from all the centuries of Hellenic song. Sappho is there, indeed, because " though her flowers were few, they were all roses," and, almost unseen, a single virginal shoot of the crocus bears the name of Erinna. That was all that womanhood gave of durable poetry to the literature of antiquity. A critic, writing five hundred years after her death, speaks of still hearing the swan-note of Erinna clear above the jangling chatter of the jays, and of still thinking those three hundred hexameter verses sung by a girl of nineteen as lovely as the loveliest of Homer's. Even at the time of the birth of Christ, Erinna's writings consisted of what could be printed on half a dozen pages of this volume. The whole of her extant work, and of Sappho's too, could now be pressed into a newspaper column. But their fame lives on, and of Sappho, at least, enough survives to prove beyond a shadow of doubt the lofty inspiration of her genius. She is the type of the woman-poet who exists not by reason of the variety or volume of her work, but by virtue of its intensity, its individuality, its artistic perfection.

At no time was it more necessary to insist on this truth than it is to-day. The multiplication of books of verse, the hackneyed character of all obvious notation of life and feeling, should, one would fancy, tend to make our poets more exiguous, more concise, and more trimly girt. There are few men nowadays from whom an immense flood of writing can be endured without fatigue ; few who can hold the trumpet to their lips for hours in the market-place without making a desert around them. Yet there never was a time when the pouring out of verse was less restrained within bounds. Everything that occurs to the poet seems, to-day, to be worth writing down and printing. The result is the neglect of really good and charming work, which misses all effect because it is drowned in stuff that is second- or third-rate. The women who write, in particular, pursued by that commercial fervour which is so curious a feature of our new literary life, and which sits so inelegantly on a female figure, are in a ceaseless hurry to work off and hurry away into oblivion those qualities of their style which might, if seriously and coyly guarded, attract a permanent attention.

Among the women who have written verse in the Victorian age there is not one by whom this reproach is less deserved than it is by Miss Rossetti. Severely true to herself, an artist of conscientiousness as high as her skill is exquisite, she has never swept her fame to sea in a flood of her own outpourings. In the following pages I desire to pay no more than a just tribute of respect to one of the most perfect poets of the age—not one of the most powerful, of course, nor one of the most epoch-making, but to one of the most perfect—to a writer toward whom we may not unreasonably expect that students of English literature in the twenty-fourth century may look back as the critics of Alexandria did toward Sappho and toward Erinna.

So much has been written, since the untimely death of Dante Gabriel Rossetti, on the circumstances of his family history, that it is not requisite to enter very fully into that subject in the present sketch of his youngest sister. It is well known that the Italian poet Gabriele Rossetti, after a series of romantic adventures endured in the cause of liberty, settled in London, and married the daughter of another Italian exile, G. Polidori, Lord Byron's physician. From this stock, three-fourths of which was purely Italian, there sprang four children, of whom Dante Gabriel was the second, and Christina Georgina, born in December 1830, the youngest. There was nothing in the training of these children which foreshadowed their various distinction in the future ; although the transplanted blood ran quicker, no doubt, in veins that must now be called English, not Italian, even as the wine-red anemone broke into flower from the earth that was carried to the Campo Santo out of Palestine.

We cannot fathom these mysteries of transplantation. No doubt a thousand Italian families might settle in London, and their children be born as deaf to melody and as blind to Nature as their playfellows long native to Hoxton or Clerkenwell. Yet it is not possible to hold it quite an accident that this thousand and first family discovered in London soil the precise chemical qualities that made its Italian fibre break into clusters of blossom. Gabriel Rossetti, both as poet and painter, remained very Italian to the last, but his sister is a thorough Englishwoman. Unless I make a great mistake, she has scarcely visited Italy, and in her poetry the landscape and the observation of Nature are not only English, they are so thoroughly local that I doubt whether there is one touch in them all which proves her to have strayed more than fifty miles from London in any direction. I have no reason for saying so beyond internal evidence, but I should be inclined to suggest that the county of Sussex alone is capable of having supplied all the imagery which Miss Rossetti's poems contain.

Her literary repertory, too, seems purely English ; there is hardly a solitary touch in her work which betrays her transalpine parentage.

In a letter to myself, in words which she kindly lets me give to the public, Miss Rossetti has thus summed up some valuable impressions of her earliest bias toward writing :

" For me, as well as for Gabriel, whilst our ' school ' was everything, it was no one definite thing. I, as the least and last of the group, may remind you that besides the clever and cultivated parents who headed us all, I in particular beheld far ahead of myself the clever sister and two clever brothers who were a little (though but a little) my seniors. And as to acquirements, I lagged out of all proportion behind them, and have never over-taken them to this day."

I interrupt my distinguished friend to remark that, even if we do not take this modest declaration with a grain of salt, it is interesting to find one more example of the fact that the possession of genius by no means presupposes a nature apt for what are called acquirements. Miss Rossetti proceeds :

" If any one thing schooled me in the direction of poetry, it was perhaps the delightful idle liberty to prowl all alone about my grandfather's cottage-grounds some thirty miles from London, entailing in my childhood a long stage - coach journey ! This privilege came to an end when I was eight years old, if not earlier. The grounds were quite small, and on the simplest scale—but in those days to me they were vast, varied, worth exploring. After those charming holidays ended I remained pent up in London till I was a great girl of fourteen, when delight reawakened at the sight of primroses in a railway cutting,—a prelude to many lovely country sights."

My impression is that a great deal of judicious neglect was practised in the Rossetti family, and that, like so many people of genius, the two poets, brother and sister, contrived to evade the educational mill. From the lips of Miss Christina herself I have it that all through her early girlhood she lay as a passive weight on the hands of those who invited her to explore those bosky groves called arithmetic, grammar, and the use of the globes. In Mr. R. L. Stevenson's little masterpiece of casuistry called *On Idlers and Idling*, he has discussed the temper of mind so sympathetically that I will say no more than this, that Philistia never will comprehend the certain fact that, to genius, Chapter VI., which is primroses in a railway cutting, is often far more important than Chapter XIII., which happens to be the subjunctive mood. But for these mysteries of education I must refer the ingenuous reader to Mr. Stevenson's delightful pages.

From her early childhood Miss Rossetti seems to have prepared herself for the occupation of her life, the art of poetry. When she was eleven her verses began to be noticed and preserved, and an extremely rare little volume, the very cynosure of Victorian bibliography, permits us to observe the development of her talent. One of the rarest of books—when it occasionally turns up at sales it commands an extravagant price—is *Verses by Christina G. Rossetti*, privately printed in 1847, at the press of her grandfather Mr. G. Polidori, " at No. 15 Park Village East, Regent's Park, London." This little volume of sixty-six pages, dedicated to the author's mother, and preceded by a pretty little preface signed by Mr. Polidori, is a curious revelation of the evolution of the poet's genius. There is hardly one piece in it which Miss Rossetti would choose to reprint in a collected edition of her works, but there are many which possess the greatest interest to a student of her mature style. The earliest verses—since all are dated—show us merely the child's desire for expression in verse, for experiment in rhyme and meter. Gradually we see the buddings of an individual manner, and in the latest piece, " The Dead City," the completion of which seems to have led to the printing of the little collection, we find the poet assuming something of her adult manner. Here are some stanzas from this rarest of booklets, which will be new, in every probability, to all my readers, and in these we detect, unmistakably, the accents of the future author of *Goblin Market* :

In green emerald baskets were
Sun-red apples, streaked and fair ;

Here the nectarine and peach,
    And ripe plum lay, and on each
The bloom rested everywhere.

Grapes were hanging overhead,
Purple, pale, and ruby-red,
    And in the panniers all around
    Yellow melons shone, fresh-found
With the dew upon them spread.

And the apricot and pear,
And the pulpy fig were there,
    Cherries and dark mulberries,
    Bunchy currants, strawberries,
And the lemon wan and fair.

By far the best and most characteristic of all her girlish verses, however, are those contained in a long piece entitled " Divine and Human Pleading," dated 1846. It is a pleasure to be the first to publish a passage which the author needs not blush to own after nearly fifty years, every stanza of which bears the stamp of her peculiar manner :

A woman stood beside his bed :
    Her breath was fragrance all ;
Round her the light was very bright,
    The air was musical.

Her footsteps shone upon the stars,
    Her robe was spotless white ;
Her breast was radiant with the Cross,
    Her head with living light.

Her eyes beamed with a sacred fire,
    And on her shoulders fair,
From underneath her golden crown,
    Clustered her golden hair.

Yet on her bosom her white hands
Were folded quietly :
Yet was her glorious head bowed low
In deep humility.

In these extracts from the volume of 1847 we
see more than the germ ; we see the imperfect
development of two qualities which have particularly characterised the poetry of Miss Rossetti
—in the first an entirely direct and vivid mode of
presenting to us the impression of richly coloured
physical objects, a feat in which she sometimes
rivals Keats and Tennyson ; and in the second a
brilliant simplicity in the conduct of episodes of
a visionary character, and a choice of expression
which is exactly in keeping with these, a sort of
Tuscan candour, as of a sacred picture in which
each saint or angel is robed in a dress of one unbroken colour.   These two qualities combined, in
spite of their apparent incompatibility—an austere
sweetness coupled with a luscious and sensuous
brightness—to form one side of Miss Rossetti's
curious poetic originality.

Three years later, in 1850, she was already a
finished poet.   That charming and pathetic failure
The Germ, a forlorn little periodical which
attempted to emanate from the new group of
Preraphaelites, as they called themselves, counted
her among its original contributors.   Her brother
Gabriel, indeed, who had already written, in its
earliest form, his remarkable poem of *The Blessed
Damozel*, was the central force and prime artificer
of the movement, which had begun about a year

before. It was a moment of transition in English poetry. The old race was dying in its last representative, Wordsworth. Mr. Tennyson, Mr. Browning, Miss Barrett were the main figures of the day, while the conscience of young men and women addicted to verse was troubled with a variety of heresies, the malignity of which is hardly to be realised by us after fifty years. Mr. Bailey's *Festus* was a real power for evil, strong enough to be a momentary snare to the feet of Tennyson in writing *Maud*, and even of Browning. A host of " Spasmodists," as they were presently called, succeeded in appalling the taste of the age with their vast and shapeless tragedies, or monodramas.

Then, with a different voice, but equally far removed from the paths of correct tradition in verse, came Clough, singing in slovenly hexameters of Oxford and the pleasures of radical undergraduates in highland bothies. Clough, with his hold on reality, and his sympathetic modern accent, troubled the Preraphaelites a little ; they were less moved by a far more pure and exquisite music, a song as of Simonides himself, which also reached them from Oxford, when Matthew Arnold, in 1849, made his first appearance with his lovely and long neglected *Strayed Reveller*. Mr. Coventry Patmore, with his *Poems* of 1844, was a recognised elder brother of their own, and almost everything else which was to be well done in verse for many years was to arise from among themselves, or in emulation of them. So that never was periodical better named than

The Germ, the seed which put forth two cotyledons, and then called itself *Art and Letters* ; and put forth two more little leaves, and then seemed to die.

Among the anonymous contributions to the first number of *The Germ*—that for January 1850 —are two which we know to be Miss Rossetti's. These are, " Where Sunless Rivers Weep," and " Love, Strong as Death, is Dead." In the February number, under the pseudonym of Ellen Alleyn, she printed " A Pause of Thought," the song, " Oh, Roses for the Flush of Youth," and " I said of Laughter, It is Vain." To the March number, then styled *Art and Letters*, Ellen Alleyn contributed a long piece called " Repining," which does not seem to have been reprinted, and " Sweet Death " (" The Sweetest Blossoms Die.") To the fourth and last number, in which an alien and far more commonplace influence may be traced than in the others, she contributed nothing. Of her seven pieces, however, printed in *The Germ* in 1850, when she was twenty, there are five (if we omit " A Pause of Thought " and " Repining ") which rank to this day among her very finest lyrics, and display her style as absolutely formed. Though the youngest poet of the confraternity, she appears indeed in *The Germ* as the most finished, and even, for the moment, the most promising, since her brother Gabriel, if the author of *The Blessed Damozel*, was also responsible for those uncouth Flemish studies in verse which he very wisely refused in later years to own or to republish.

CHRISTINA ROSSETTI

Time passed, and the obscure group of boys and girls who called themselves Preraphaelites found themselves a centre of influence and curiosity. In poetry, as in painting and sculpture, they conquered, and more readily, perhaps, in their pupils than in themselves. The first independent publications of the school, at least, came from visitors who had been children in 1850. These books were scarcely noticed by the public; if Mr. Morris's *Defence of Guinevere* attracted a few readers in 1858, Mr. Swinburne's *Queen Mother* fell stillborn from the press in 1860. These prepared the way for real and instantaneous successes—for Miss Rossetti's *Goblin Market* in 1862, for Mr Woolner's *My Beautiful Lady* in 1863, for Mr. Swinburne's dazzling *Atalanta in Calydon* in 1865. At last, in 1870, there tardily appeared, after such expectation and tiptoe curiosity as have preceded no other book in our generation, the *Poems* of Gabriel Rossetti.

It is with these poets that Miss Rossetti takes her historical position, and their vigour and ambition had a various influence upon her style. On this side there can be no doubt that association with men so learned and eager, so daring in experiment, so well equipped in scholarship, gave her an instant and positive advantage. By nature she would seem to be of a cloistered and sequestered temper, and her genius was lifted on this wave of friendship to heights which it would not have dreamed of attempting alone. On the other hand, it is possible that, after the first moment, this association with the strongest male talent of the time has not been favourable to public appreciation of her work. Critics have taken for granted that she was a satellite, and have been puzzled to notice her divergences from the type. Of these divergences the most striking is the religious one. Neither Gabriel Rossetti, nor Mr. Swinburne, nor Mr. Morris has shown any sympathy with, or any decided interest in, the tenets of Protestantism. Now Miss Christina Rossetti's poetry is not merely Christian and Protestant, it is Anglican ; nor her divine works only, but her secular also, bear the stamp of uniformity with the doctrines of the Church of England.

What is very interesting in her poetry is the union of this fixed religious faith with a hold upon physical beauty and the richer parts of Nature which allies her with her brother and with their younger friends. She does not shrink from strong delineation of the pleasures of life even when she is denouncing them. In one of the most austere of her sacred pieces, she describes the Children of the World in these glowing verses :

> Milk-white, wine-flushed, among the vines,
> Up and down leaping, to and fro,
> Most glad, most full, made strong with wines,
> Blooming as peaches pearled with dew,
> Their golden windy hair afloat,
> Love-music warbling in their throat,
> Young men and women come and go.

There is no literary hypocrisy here, no pretence that the apple of life is full of ashes ; and this gives a startling beauty, the beauty of artistic contrast, to the poet's studies in morality. Miss Rossetti, indeed, is so didactic in the undercurrent of her mind, so anxious to adorn her tale with a religious moral, that she needs all her art, all her vigorous estimate of physical loveliness, to make her poetry delightful as poetry. That she does make it eminently delightful merely proves her extraordinary native gift. The two long pieces she has written, her two efforts at a long breath, are sustained so well as to make us regret that she has not put out her powers in the creation of a still more complete and elaborated composition. Of these two poems *Goblin Market* is by far the more popular ; the other, *The Prince's Progress*, which appeared in 1866, has never attracted such attention as it deserves.

It is not necessary to describe a poem so well known to every lover of verse as *Goblin Market*. It is one of the very few purely fantastic poems of recent times which have really kept up the old tradition of humoresque literature. Its witty and fantastic conception is embroidered with fancies, descriptions, peals of laughing music, which clothe it as a queer Japanese figure may be clothed with brocade, so that the entire effect at last is beautiful and harmonious without ever having ceased to be grotesque. I confess that while I dimly perceive the underlying theme to be a didactic one, and nothing less than the sacrifice of self by a sister to recuperate a sister's virtue, I cannot follow the parable through all its delicious episodes. Like a Japanese work of art, again, one perceives the general intention, and one is satisfied with the beauty of all the detail, without comprehending or wishing to comprehend every part of the execution. For instance, the wonderful scene in which Lizzie sits beleaguered by the goblins, and receives with hard-shut mouth all the syrups that they squeeze against her skin—this from the point of view of poetry is perfect, and needs no apology or commentary; but its place in the parable it would, surely, be extremely hard to find. It is, therefore, astonishing to me that the general public, that strange and unaccountable entity, has chosen to prefer *Goblin Market*, which we might conceive to be written for poets alone, to *The Prince's Progress*, where the parable and the teaching are as clear as noonday. The prince is a handsome, lazy fellow, who sets out late upon his pilgrimage, loiters in bad company by the way, is decoyed by light loves, and the hope of life, and the desire of wealth, and reaches his destined bride at last, only to find her dead. This has an obvious moral, but it is adorned with verse of the very highest romantic beauty. Every claim which criticism has to make for the singular merit of Miss Rossetti might be substantiated from this little-known romance, from which I must resist the pleasure of quoting more than a couple of stanzas descriptive of daybreak :

> At the death of night and the birth of day,
> When the owl left off his sober play,

98

And the bat hung himself out of the way,—
　Woke the song of mavis and merle,
And heaven put off its hodden grey
　For mother-o'-pearl.

Peeped up daises here and there,
Here, there, and everywhere ;
Rose a hopeful lark in the air,
　Spreading out towards the sun his breast ;
While the moon set solemn and fair
　Away in the West.

With the apparent exceptions of *Goblin Market* and *The Prince's Progress*, both of which indeed are of a lyrical nature, Miss Rossetti has written only lyrics. All poets are unequal, except the bad ones, who are uniformly bad. Miss Rossetti indulges in the privilege which Wordsworth, Burns, and so many great masters have enjoyed, of writing extremely flat and dull poems at certain moments, and of not perceiving that they are dull or flat. She does not err in being mediocre ; her lyrics are bad or good, and the ensuing remarks deal with that portion only of her poems with which criticism is occupied in surveying work so admirably original as hers, namely, that which is worthy of her reputation. Her lyrics, then, are eminent for their glow of colouring, their vivid and novel diction, and for a certain penetrating accent, whether in joy or pain, which rivets the attention. Her habitual tone is one of melancholy reverie, the pathos of which is strangely intensified by her appreciation of beauty and pleasure. There is not a chord of the minor key in " A Birthday,"

and yet the impression which its cumulative
ecstasy leaves upon the nerves is almost pathetic :

> My heart is like a singing-bird
>   Whose nest is in a watered shoot ;
> My heart is like an apple-tree
>   Whose boughs are bent with thick-set fruit ;
> My heart is like a rainbow-shell
>   That paddles in a halcyon sea ;
> My heart is gladder than all these
>   Because my love is come to me.
>
> Raise me a dais of silk and down ;
>   Hang it with vair and purple dyes :
> Carve it in doves and pomegranates,
>   And peacocks with a hundred eyes ;
> Work it in gold and silver grapes,
>   In leaves and silver fleurs-de-lys ;
> Because the birthday of my life
>   Is come, my love is come to me.

It is very rarely, indeed, that the poet strikes so
jubilant a note as this. Her customary music is
sad, often poignantly sad. Her lyrics have that
desiderium, that obstinate longing for something
lost out of life, which Shelley's have, although her
Christian faith gives her regret a more resigned
and sedate character than his possesses. In the
extremely rare gift of song-writing Miss Rossetti
has been singularly successful. Of the poets of
our time she stands next to Lord Tennyson in
this branch of the art, in the spontaneous and
complete quality of her *lieder*, and in their
propriety for the purpose of being sung. At
various times this art has flourished in our race ;
eighty years ago, most of the poets could write

songs, but it is almost a lost art in our generation.
The songs of our living poets are apt to be over-
polished or under-polished, so simple as to be
bald, or else so elaborate as to be wholly unsuitable
for singing. But such a song as this is not unworthy to be classed with the melodies of Shakespeare, of Burns, of Shelley :

> Oh, roses for the flush of youth,
>   And laurel for the perfect prime ;
> But pluck an ivy-branch for me
>   Grown old before my time.
>
> Oh, violets for the grave of youth,
>   And bay for those dead in their prime ;
> Give me the withered leaves I chose
>   Before in the old time.

Her music is very delicate, and it is no small
praise to her that she it is who, of living verse-
writers, has left the strongest mark on the metrical
nature of that miraculous artificer of verse, Mr.
Swinburne. In his *Poems and Ballads*, as other
critics have long ago pointed out, as was shown
when that volume first appeared, several of Miss
Rossetti's discoveries were transferred to his more
scientific and elaborate system of harmonies, and
adapted to more brilliant effects. The reader of
Mr. Swinburne would judge that of all his
immediate contemporaries Miss Rossetti and the
late Mr. FitzGerald, the translator of *Omar
Khayyám*, had been those who had influenced
his style the most. Miss Rossetti, however, makes
no pretence to elaborate metrical effects ; she is

even sometimes a little naïve, a little careless, in her rough, rhymeless endings, and metrically her work was better in her youth than it has been since.

The sonnets present points of noticeable interest. They are few, but they are of singular excellence. They have this peculiarity, that many of them are objective. Now the great bulk of good sonnets is purely subjective—occupied with reverie, with regret, with moral or religious enthusiasm. Even the celebrated sonnets of Gabriel Rossetti will be found to be mainly subjective. On the question of the relative merit of the sonnets of the brother and the sister, I hold a view in which I believe that few will at present coincide; I am certain Miss Rossetti herself will not. If she honours me by reading these pages, she may possibly recollect a conversation, far more important to me of course than to her, which we held in 1870, soon after I had first the privilege of becoming known to her. I was venturing to praise her sonnets, when she said, with the sincerity of evident conviction, that they "could only be admired before Gabriel, by printing his in the *Fortnightly Review*, showed the source of their inspiration." I was sure then, and I am certain now, that she was wrong. The sonnets are not the product of, they do not even bear any relation to those of, her brother.

Well do I recollect the publication of these sonnets of Gabriel Rossetti, in 1869, when, at a moment when curiosity regarding the mysterious painter-poet was at its height, they suddenly blossomed forth in a certain number of the *Fortnightly Review*, in whose solemn pages we were wont to see nothing lighter or more literary than esoteric politics and the prose mysteries of positivism. We were dazzled by their Italian splendour of phraseology, amazed that such sonorous anapests, that such a burst of sound, should be caged within the sober limits of the sonnet, fascinated by the tenderness of the long-drawn amorous rhetoric ; but there were some of us who soon recovered an equilibrium of taste, in which it seemed that the tradition of the English sonnet, its elegance of phrase, its decorum of movement, were too rudely displaced by this brilliant Italian intruder, and that underneath the melody and the glowing diction, the actual thought, the valuable and intelligible residue of poetry, was too often much more thin than Rossetti allowed it to be in the best of his other poems. As to Gabriel Rossetti's sonnets being his own best work, as has been asserted, I for one must entirely and finally disagree. I believe that of all his poetry they form the section which will be the first to tarnish. Quite otherwise is it with Miss Christina Rossetti. It is in certain of her objective sonnets that her touch is most firm and picturesque, her intelligence most weighty, and her style most completely characteristic. The reader need but turn to " After Death," " On the Wing," " Venus's Looking-Glass " (in the volume of 1875), and the marvellous " A Triad " [1] to con-

---

[1] Why has Miss Rossetti allowed this piece, one of the gems of the volume of 1862, to drop out of her collected poems ?

cede the truth of this ; while in the more obvious
subjective manner of sonnet-writing she is one of
the most successful poets of our time. In " The
World," where she may be held to come closest to
her brother as a sonneteer, she seems to me to
surpass him.

From the first a large section of Miss Rossetti's
work has been occupied with sacred and devotional
themes. Through this most rare and difficult
department of the art, which so few essay without
breaking on the Scylla of doctrine on the one hand,
or being whirled in the Charybdis of commonplace
dullness on the other, she has steered with extraordinary success. Her sacred poems are truly
sacred, and yet not unpoetical. As a religious
poet of our time she has no rival but Cardinal
Newman, and it could only be schismatic prejudice
or absence of critical faculty which should deny her
a place, as a poet, higher than that of our exquisite
master of prose. To find her exact parallel it is
at once her strength and her snare that we must
go back to the middle of the seventeenth century.
She is the sister of George Herbert ; she is of the
family of Crashaw, of Vaughan, of Wither. The
metrical address of Herbert has been perilously
attractive to her ; the broken stanzas of " Consider " or of " Long Barren " remind us of the age
when pious aspirations took the form of wings, or
hour-glasses, or lamps of the temple. The most
thrilling and spirited of her sacred poems have
been free from these Marini-like subtleties. There
is only what is best in the quaint and fervent school

of Herbert visible in such pieces as " The Three
Enemies," " A Rose Plant in Jericho," " Passing
Away, saith the World," and " Up Hill." Still
more completely satisfactory, perhaps, is " Amor
Mundi," first included in the *Poems* of 1875,
which takes rank as one of the most solemn,
imaginative, and powerful lyrics on a purely
religious subject ever printed in England.

These critical and biographical remarks were
mainly written in 1882, but not printed until 1893.
They were undertaken at the suggestion of Dante
Gabriel Rossetti, who was kind enough to consider
that I had an appreciation of his sister such as is
more common now than fourteen years ago. They
were scarcely finished when the news came of his
death, and in the agitation produced by that event,
I thought it better to put aside for a time my
criticism of Christina.

It will, perhaps, be not inappropriate for me to
record here my few personal recollections of this
illustrious lady. It was not my privilege to meet
her more than some dozen times in the flesh, and
those times mainly in the winter of 1870–71. But
on most of those occasions I had the good fortune
to converse with her for a long while ; and up to a
few months before her death we corresponded at
not particularly distant intervals. She is known
to the world, and very happily known, by her
brother's portraits of her, and in particular by the
singularly beautiful chalk drawing in profile, dated

1866. I think that tasteful arrangement of dress might have made her appear a noble and even a romantic figure so late as 1870, but, as I suppose, an ascetic or almost methodistical reserve caused her to clothe herself in a style, or with an absence of style, which was really distressing ; her dark hair was streaked across her olive forehead, and turned up in a chignon ; the high stiff dress ended in a hard collar and plain brooch, the extraordinarily ordinary skirt sank over a belated crinoline, and these were inflictions hard to bear from the high-priestess of Preraphaelitism. When it is added that her manner, from shyness, was of a portentous solemnity, that she had no small talk whatever, and that the common topics of the day appeared to be entirely unknown to her, it will be understood that she was considered highly formidable by the young and the flighty. I have seen her sitting alone, in the midst of a noisy drawing-room, like a pillar of cloud, a Sibyl whom no one had the audacity to approach.

Yet a kinder or simpler soul, or one less concentrated on self, or of a humbler sweetness, never existed. And to an enthusiast, who broke the bar of conventional chatter, and ventured on real subjects, her heart seemed to open like an unsealed fountain. The heavy lids of her weary-looking, bistred, Italian eyes would lift and display her ardour as she talked of the mysteries of poetry and religion. My visits to her, in her mother's house, 56 Euston Square, were abruptly brought to a close. On May 1, 1871, I received a note from her elder sister Maria warning me not to dine with them on the following Tuesday, as her sister was suddenly and alarmingly ill. This was, in fact, the mysterious complaint which thenceforth kept Christina bedridden, and sometimes at the point of death, for two years. She recovered, but the next time I saw her—she was well enough to be working in the British Museum in the summer of 1873—she was so strangely altered as to be scarcely recognisable.

By degrees, to my great satisfaction, Miss Christina came to look upon me as in some little sense her champion in the press. " The pen you use for me has always a soft rather than a hard nib," she said, and in truth, whenever I found an opportunity of praising her pure and admirable poems, I was not slow to employ it. That I was not exempt, however, from an occasional peck even from this gentlest of turtle-doves, a letter (written in December 1875) reminds me. I had reviewed somewhere the first collected edition of her *Poems*, and I had ventured to make certain reservations. There are some points of valuable self-analysis which make a part of this letter proper to be quoted here :

" Save me from my friends ! You are certainly up in your subject, and as I *might* have fared worse in other hands I will not regret that rival reviewer [Mr. Theodore Watts] who was hindered from saying his say. As to the lamented early lyrics, I do not suppose myself to be the person least tenderly reminiscent of them [I had grumbled at the excision of some admirable favourites] ; but it at any rate appears to be the commoner fault amongst verse-writers to write what is not worth writing, than to suppress what would merit hearers. I for my part am a great believer in the genuine poetic impulse belonging (very often) to the spring and not to the autumn of life, and some established reputations fail to shake me in this opinion ; at any rate, if so one feels the possibility to stand in one's own case, then I vote that the grace of silence succeed the grace of song. By all which I do not bind myself to unbroken silence, but meanwhile I defend my position—or, you may retort, I do not defend it. By-the-by, your *upness* does not prevent my protesting that Edith and Maggie did not dream or even nap ; *Flora* did ; but have I not caught *you* napping ? Do, pray, come and see me and we will not fight."

It is difficult to speak of either of the Rossetti ladies without a reference to the elder sister, whom also I had the privilege of knowing in early days. She left upon me the impression of stronger character, though of narrower intellect and infinitely poorer imagination. I formed the idea, I know not whether with justice, that the pronounced high-church views of Maria, who throve on ritual, starved the less pietistic, but painfully conscientious nature of Christina. The influence of Maria Francesca Rossetti on her sister seemed to be like that of Newton upon Cowper, a species of police surveillance exercised by a hard, convinced mind over a softer and more fanciful one. Miss Maria Rossetti, who generally needed the name of Dante to awaken her from a certain social torpor, died in 1876, but not until she had set her seal on the religious habits of her sister. Such, at least, was the notion which I formed, perhaps on slight premises.

That the conscience of the younger sister was, in middle life, so tender as to appear almost morbid, no one, I think, will deny. I recall an amusing instance of it. In the winter of 1874, I was asked to secure some influential signatures to a petition against the destruction of a part of the New Forest. Mr. Swinburne promised me his, if I could induce Miss Christina Rossetti to give hers, suggesting as he did so, that the feat might not be an easy one. In fact, I found that no little palaver was necessary; but at last she was so far persuaded of the innocence of the protest that she wrote *Chr*; she then stopped, dropped the pen, and said very earnestly, " Are you sure that they do not propose to build churches on the land ? " After a long time, I succeeded in convincing her that such a scheme was not thought of, and she proceeded to write *istina G. Ros*, and stopped again. " Nor school-houses ? " fluctuating with tremulous scruple. At length she finished the signature, and I carried the parchment off to claim the fulfilment of Mr. Swinburne's promise. And the labourer felt that he was worthy of his hire.

On the 6th of July 1876, I saw Christina Rossetti for the last time. I suppose that her life, during the last twenty years of it, was as sequestered as that of any pious woman in a religious house. She stirred but little, I fancy, from her rooms save to attend the services of the Anglican church. That her mind continued humane and simple her successive publications and her kind and sometimes playful letters proved. Misfortunes attended her family, and she who had been the centre of so eager and vivid a group, lived to find herself almost solitary. At length, on the 29th of December 1894, after prolonged sufferings borne with infinite patience, this great writer, who was also a great saint, passed into the region of her visions.

A FIRST SIGHT OF TENNYSON

A FIRST SIGHT OF TENNYSON

THERE is a reaction in the popular feeling about Tennyson, and I am told that upon the young he has lost his hold, which was like that of an octopus upon us in my salad days. These revolutions in taste do not trouble me much ; they are inevitable and they are not final. But those who " cannot read " " Maud " and " In Memoriam " to-day must take it on the word of a veteran that forty years ago we, equally, could not help reading them. There was a revolt against the tyranny now and then ; in particular, after " The Loves of the Wrens " and " Enoch Arden " a rather serious mutiny broke out among Tennyson's admirers, but " Lucretius " appeared and we were enslaved again.

It is strange to look back upon the unrestrained panegyric which took the place of the higher criticism of Tennyson in the closing years of the nineteenth century. When a very clever man like the late Duke of Argyll, a man of sober years, could say, without being reproached, that Tennyson's blank verse in the *Idylls* was sweeter and stronger than " the stately march of Elizabethan English in its golden prime"; when Mr. Gladstone could declare of Arthur in the same *Idylls* that he " knew not where to look in history or letters for a nobler or more overpowering conception of man as he might be," then a reaction, however tenderly delayed, was inevitable. The uncritical note of praise is almost more surely hurtful to a reputation than the uncritical note of blame, for it makes a wound that it is much harder to heal. Tennyson is now suffering from the extravagant obsequiousness of his late Victorian admirers. At the moment of which I am about to speak, Tennyson had published nothing since " The Holy Grail," and it was understood that he was slightly startled by the arrival of Swinburne, Morris, and the Rossettis on a stage which he, with Robert Browning still very much in the background, had hitherto sufficiently filled. But the vogue of these new-comers was confined to the elect. In the world at large Tennyson was the English living poet *par excellence*, great by land and great by sea, the one survivor of the heroic chain of masters.

It was the early summer of 1871, and I was palely baking, like a crumpet, in a singularly horrible underground cage, made of steel bars, called the Den. This was a place such as no responsible being is allowed to live in nowadays, where the transcribers on the British Museum staff were immured in a half-light. This cellar was prominently brought forward a year or two later in the course of a Royal Commission on the British Museum, being " lifted into notice " only to be absolutely condemned by the indignation of the medical faculty. I was dolefully engaged here, being then one of the humblest of mankind, a

A FIRST SIGHT OF TENNYSON

Junior Assistant in the Printed Books Department of the British Museum, on some squalid task, in what was afterwards described by a witness as an atmosphere " scented with rotten morocco, and an indescribable odour familiar in foreign barracks," when a Senior Assistant, one of the rare just spirits in that academical Dotheboys Hall, W. R. S. Ralston, came dashing down the flights of curling steel staircase, to the danger of his six feet six of height, and of the beard that waved down to his waist. Over me he bent, and in a whisper (we were forbidden to speak out loud in the Den) he said, " Come up stairs at once and be presented to Mr. Tennyson ! "

Proud young spirits of the present day, for whom life opens in adulation, will find it scarcely possible to realise what such a summons meant to me. As we climbed those steep and spiral staircases towards light and day, my heart pounded in my chest with agitation. The feeling of excitement was almost overwhelming : it was not peculiar to myself ; such ardours were common in those years. Some day a philosopher must analyse it—that enthusiasm of the seventies, that intoxicating belief in " the might of poesy." Tennyson was scarcely a human being to us, he was the God of the Golden Bow ; I approached him now like a blank idiot about to be slain, " or was I a worm, too low-crawling for death, O Delphic Apollo ? " It is not merely that no person living now calls forth that kind of devotion, but the sentiment of mystery has disappeared.

Not genius itself could survive the kodak snap-shots and the halfpenny newspapers.

It must, I suppose, have been one of those days on which the public was then excluded, since we found Tennyson, with a single companion, alone in what was then the long First Sculpture Gallery. His friend was James Spedding, at whom in other conditions I should have gazed with interest, but in the Delphic presence he was not visible to my dazzled eyes. Mr. Thornycroft's statue of the poet, now placed in Trinity College, gives an admirable impression of him at a slightly later date than 1871, if (that is) it is translated out of terms of white into terms of black. Tennyson, at that time, was still one of the darkest of men, as he is familiarly seen in all his earlier portraits. But those portraits do not give, although Mr. Thornycroft has suggested, the singular majesty of his figure, standing in repose. Ralston, for all his six feet six, seemed to dwindle before this magnificent presence, while Tennyson stood, bare-headed among the Roman Emperors, every inch as imperial-looking as the best of them. He stood there as we approached him, very still, with slightly drooping eyelids, and made no movement, no gesture of approach. When I had been presented, and had shaken his hand, he continued to consider me in a silence which would have been deeply disconcerting if it had not, somehow, seemed kindly, and even, absurd as it sounds, rather shy.

The stillness was broken by Ralston's irrele-vantly mentioning that I was presently to start for Norway. The bard then began to talk about that country, which I was surprised to find he had visited some dozen years before. Ralston kindly engaged Spedding in conversation, so that Tennyson might now apply himself to me ; with infinite goodness he did so, even " making conversation," for I was hopelessly tongue-tied, and must, in fact, have cut a very poor figure. Tennyson, it miraculously appeared, had read some of my stammering verses, and was vaguely gracious about them. He seemed to accept me as a sheep in the fold of which he was, so magnificently, the shepherd. This completed my undoing, but he did not demand from me speech. He returned to the subject of Norway, and said it was not the country for him to travel in, since you could only travel in it in funny little round carts, called *karjols*, which you must drive yourself, and that he was far too near-sighted for that. (I had instantly wondered at his double glasses, of a kind I had never seen before.)

Then somebody suggested that we should examine the works of art, which, in that solitude, we could delightfully do. Tennyson led us, and we stopped at any sculpture which attracted his notice. But the only remark which my memory has retained was made before the famous black bust of Antinous. Tennyson bent forward a little, and said, in his deep slow voice, " Ah ! this is the inscrutable Bithynian ! " There was a pause, and then he added, gazing into the eyes of the bust : " If we knew what he knew, we should understand the ancient world." If I live to be a hundred years old, I shall still hear his rich tones as he said this, without emphasis, without affectation, as though he were speaking to himself. And soon after, the gates of heaven were closed, and I went down three flights of stairs to my hell of rotten morocco.

THE LAST OF THE PAGANS

THE LAST OF THE PAGANS

THREE hundred years after great poetry had seemed to cease in Italy, an exile from Egypt revived it during ten years of superb production. The writings of Claudian have not been very easy of access, the latest edition of the Latin text being one published in Leipzig thirty years ago, nor was there till now any translation in English except that issued at Sherborne in 1817 by a certain A. Hawkins, in heroic couplets, very dead and dreary, and none the livelier for being verbally rather close to the original. Hence inclusion of the great Milanese poet in the Loeb Library is particularly welcome, if only because Claudian is invaluable to historians.

It would be impertinent in me to appraise Mr. Maurice Platnauer's scholarship, but there is evident in his whole apparatus—his translation in prose, his manipulation of the text, his notes and his bibliography—an admirable competency. There is now no excuse for not reading the last of the ancients, of whom Gibbon said that " he was endowed with the rare and precious talent of raising the meanest, of adorning the most barren, and of diversifying the most similar topics." It is in the capacity of a lantern of information throwing radiance on the intrigues of a particularly obscure period of late Latin history, that Claudian has been chiefly examined. Historians, from Gibbon to Thomas Hodgkin, have revelled in his records, although the first-mentioned is careful to guard us against prejudice and violence in the partisan poet. I do not know why it is that Mr. Platnauer never once quotes Gibbon, whose brilliant thirtieth chapter is full of eloquent tributes to the genius and memory of Claudian.

On one point only I venture, very timorously, to find fault with Mr. Platnauer. His performance of his task can have been attended with very little pleasure, since he seems to have no appreciation of the literary talent of Claudian. He talks about finding it " hard to withhold admiration " from the poet, but, nevertheless, he does withhold it. He says that his " faults are easy to find," and then proceeds to draw up a formidable list of them. He prints not one sentence in which there is any hearty praise of Claudian's poetry. Mr. Mackail, who has written on the subject too briefly, but with exquisite discernment, has praised in Claudian " a dignity and pathos that are worthy of the large manner of the classical period." This must disturb Mr. Platnauer, who would equally demur to Gibbon's praise of Claudian's " copious fancy. easy and sometimes forcible expression, and perpetual flow of harmonious versification." The disinclination of grammatical scholars to allow any pleasure to be taken in the works of the latest Latin authors is very curious. It is probably founded on a scholastic notion that it is bad for the young to read any

Latin that is not of the most austere Augustan purity.

The objections, however, that are brought against the authors of the Decline are frequently based not on their individual genius, but on the passage of time. A certain effort is required to realise that Claudian was separated from Juvenal, whom we may consider as the latest " classic " writer of Rome, by a period of three hundred years—that is to say, that the elder was as remote from the younger as Shakespeare is from Mr. Kipling. During those centuries modifications were introduced not merely into the language, but into the manners of life and habits of thought of Italian society. The habit of literature may have become almost extinct. But it seems the mere tyranny of a pedagogue to forbid admiration of an author simply because the style of that author bears the stamp of his own age. To refuse to recognise in Claudian a poet of a high order, the culminating point in a revival of brilliant accomplishment, and the most prominent literary feature of an epoch, is to sacrifice too much to the dignity of public school tradition.

It would seem that Claudius Claudianus was born at Canopus—that is to say, in Egypt—about the year 370. Nothing is known of him till he arrives, at perhaps the age of twenty-five, in Rome, towards 394 or 395. Hitherto it seems that he had written in Greek, but he shows himself to possess, from the first, a wonderful mastery of Latin. The poems he has left us, no doubt mere fragments of an immense poetical activity, bear the stamp of having been written between 395 and 405. This is not the place in which to dwell on the momentous events of this period in the stricken Empires of the East and of the West.

Those readers whose curiosity is stimulated by Mr. Platnauer's excellently concise account of the historical situation can gratify it by re-reading Gibbon's stately chapter on the Revolt of the Goths, or the still fuller history by the late Mr. Hodgkin. Claudian had probably just transferred himself to Milan when the Emperor Theodosius died (January 17, 395), and he was no doubt already in favour with Stilicho, the general who appears at this moment of crisis like a god out of a machine. It was Stilicho who defended Italy against the invasion of the Huns, and who presided at the final and permanent division of the Empire under Arcadius and Honorius, the young sons of the deceased Emperor. It was a new world. As Gibbon says, " the spirit of Rome expired with Theodosius," but it came precariously to life again at Milan, where Honorius reigned and Stilicho ruled, and where Claudian, with extraordinary rapidity, rose to the highest honours in the State.

What were the style and temper of the new laureate may be discerned in his earliest surviving poem, the " Panegyric on Probinus and Olybrius." It has been observed that this has " no appearance of being a first effort," and doubtless Claudian had already written, and perhaps published, much

124

that is lost. The wonder is that anything has survived. He begins with concentrated elegance, in the Alexandrian manner, by an appeal to the Sun, and there follows a beautiful passage, perhaps too artificially dragged in, about the Moon outshining the constellations. Then he expatiates in praise of the two consular brothers, who were quite young, and of Probus, their father.

What Mr. Mackail calls the " epical " manner of Claudian is illustrated by the way contemporary history is introduced. The love of Claudian for set pictures is evident in a piece displaying the two young Consuls, holding their sceptres and wrapped in their jewelled togas, as they call up Father Tiber from his oozy couch of sedge. There is a gorgeous scene where the Nymphs prepare tables set with gems in a watery palace, blazing with purple and gold. The scene closes with the ardent determination of the Hours to inscribe the names of the young Consuls on a garland of immortal blossoms, the whole being a tissue of fact and fancy that evidently dazzled the court, although to us it may seem artificial and metallic.

It is a very different Claudian who reveals himself in the satires which take up a large place in his surviving works. There can be no doubt that the diatribes against Rufinus and against Eutropius, published when those determined enemies of Stilicho had just fallen, produced an immense sensation. The Satire on Rufinus, that hypocritical creature of Theodosius, begins with a wild cry of triumph over the death of the oppressor.

Python has fallen, laid low by the arrow of Phœbus, while the whole world shouted for joy, and Cephisus, which so often foamed with his poisonous venom, now flows pure and limpid. This rapture is justified by a catalogue of the crimes of Rufinus, who does, in fact, appear to have offered a remarkably offensive type of the low-born upstart. The poet is well acquainted with the life-history of his detestable hero, and he is careful that every image and trope shall add contempt to the wretched fallen figure of Stilicho's worst enemy : then he turns abruptly to an ecstatic eulogy of Stilicho himself. With Claudian there are no fine shades ; white is snow-white and black is lamp-black.

If we take for granted that in this case blame and praise were alike deserved, the " Rufinus " is a fine example of legitimate satire, aimed at the chastisement of vice. It is not unworthy to be matched against " Absolom and Achitophel." The " Eutropius," on the other hand, is so distempered by passion as to be little better than a venomous lampoon. The poet's horror at the crimes of the court of Constantinople is unfeigned, but it is also unmeasured, and in this satire Claudian passes beyond the bounds of what is allowed even to political invective. Nor does there seem to me to be anything in the " Eutropius " so admirably written as the close of the first book of the " Rufinus," where the apotheosis of the Western world, flushing with ecstasy in hues of paradise, under the sacrificial sway of Honorius, is related in verse which is melody itself

THE LAST OF THE PAGANS

The most impersonal of Claudian's poems is that which Mr. Platnauer prints last in the collection. " The Rape of Proserpine " has not found much favour with the critics, against whose professional censure I am not anxious to pit my amateur opinion. Even Mr. Mackail, who has written more warmly of Claudian than anyone else, finds this piece a little " chilly and colourless." Yet the poet wrote it, for he says so, out of a full heart, violently moved by the majesty of an ancient exquisite story. He seems to have been acquainted with Sicily, and to have witnessed an eruption of Etna. That the style is Alexandrian is so obvious that German scholiasts have suggested that Claudian wrote it in Greek, and translated it into Latin. I do not see that there is any evidence of this. His genius was Egyptian, but we might as well conjecture that Mr. Conrad wrote his novels in Polish, and translated them into English.

" The Rape of Proserpine " presents a series of magnificent pictures, beginning with the king of Hell gloomy on his squalid throne, and culminating in the goddess among the flowers of the meadow, where Zephyr conjures Henna to welcome her with brighter roses, more azure hyacinths and violets purpler and sweeter than earth ever saw before. The soil of Sicily is all a dream-land of splendour and perfume. Proserpine is borne away after the earthquake, and is received by Pluto in an address which, it seems to me, is of a high order of poetry, full of a sort of royal tenderness, prodigal

127

and flushed. " Think not thou has lost the light of day; other stars are mine and other courses; a purer light shalt thou see, a richer age, a golden race." And then, in the soft melody of the incomparable hexameters, Hell becomes like Earth, and Hesperus shines out in a twilight sky, propitious over the silent under-world.

Perhaps the best parallel to such poetry is that of the great Scottish writers of the fifteenth century. Theirs also is a stumbling-block to critics, who are shocked at the loaded palette and " aureate " profusion of Dunbar, with its heaped-up colours and rainbow effects. No doubt, if we are possessed by the exclusive fallacy of the Romanticists, this gorgeous density of style repels us. It lacks, we are told, simplicity. But all things are not necessarily simple, and De Quincey reminded us long ago that simplicity was misplaced in a description of Sennacherib's Feast.

I do not think it has been observed how much Claudian's more splendid passages resemble the ornate style of Tennyson's old age. Some of " The Rape of Proserpine " might almost be taken out of " The Voyage of Maeldune." Compare the description of the crag of Etna towering up out of the cataract of crocus and daffodil—*ferratus lascivit apex*—with the scene in the Isle of Flowers where

the whole isle-side flashed down from the peak without ever a
    tree,
swept like a torrent of gems from the sky to the blue of the
    sea,

and it is hard not to believe that the English poet remembered his Milanese predecessor.

If splendour, if a prodigal profusion of radiant mythological reminiscence, is not to be frowned upon as dissolute and extravagant, the rapturous pictorial abundance of Claudian's fancy must be allowed its own meed of praise. " As a poet Claudian is not *always* despicable," says Mr. Platnauer. I should suppose not, indeed ! But when we read him we ought not be thinking about Burns, nor even about Horace, for there are many rooms in the house of Apollo.

The isolation of Claudian must strike the literary student with surprise. He appears like an obelisk rising from a plain ; we see him without predecessor, without contemporaries, without disciples. But this must be the result of accident, for he cannot have flourished in so complete a solitude. His poems are all addressed to a cultivated audience, evidently ready to seize every refinement of allusion and every delicacy of execution. The survival of the inscription, which once ran below his vanished statue set up by Arcadius and Honorius in the Forum of Trajan, throws a curious flash of light over the darkness. We are told on this illusive memorial that Claudian was " above all a poet and the most famous of poets," yet this tablet and the text of a few of his writings are all that remain to testify to the elaborate culture of Northern Italy before it was engulfed in the onset of the Barbarians.

A NUN'S LOVE LETTERS

A NUN'S LOVE LETTERS

BRIEF and unobtrusive as was the volume of *Lettres Portugaises* published in Paris in 1669, it exercised an influence on the sentimental literature of Europe which was very extraordinary, and to which we have not yet ceased to be subject. Since the revival of learning there had been no collection of documents dealing with the experiences of emotion in which an element of Renaissance feeling had not shown itself in some touch of rhetoric, in some flower of ornament, in some trick of language that concealed what it desired to expose. The *Portuguese Letters*, slight as they were, pleased instantly and universally because they were entirely modern. The seventeenth century, especially in France, had cultivated epistolary literature with care, even with too much care. There had been letter-writers by profession, and the value of their correspondence has been weighed and found wanting. Even in England, where the French were held up as models of letter-writing, there were not wanting critics. Howell wrote in 1625 :

" Others there are among our next transmarine neighbours eastward, who write in their own language, but their style is so soft and easy that their letters may be said to be like bodies of loose flesh without sinews ; they have neither joints of art nor arteries in them. They have a kind of simpering and lank hectic expression, made up of a bombast of words and finical affected compliments only. I cannot well away with such fleasy stuff, with such cobweb compositions, where there is no strength of matter—nothing for the reader to carry away with him that may enlarge the notions of his soul."

We may be quite sure that Howell had Balzac in his eye when he wrote this passage, and to Balzac presently succeeded Voiture. To the qualities of Voiture's famous correspondence, to its emptiness, flatness, and rhetorical elegance, signifying nothing and telling us nothing, M Gaston Boissier has lately dedicated a very amusing page of criticism. Even in the middle of the seventeenth century the French were conscious of their deficiency as letter-writers, and were anxious to remove it. Mademoiselle de Scudéry, who was as awkward as the best of them, saw that girls ought to know how to express their feelings briefly, plainly, and sincerely. In the depths of the wilderness of *Clélie* may still be found rules for letter-writing. But the time was not quite ripe, and it is noticeable that it was just before the publication of the *Portuguese Letters* that Mademoiselle, in the agonies of her grotesque passion, turned over the pages of Corneille for phrases which might express the complex emotions of her heart. If she had waited a few months a manual of the tender passion would have lain at her hand. At all events, the power to analyse the feelings in simple language, to chronicle the minute symptoms of emotion with-

out rhetoric, closely succeeds the great success of
these letters ; nor is it unworthy of notice that they
appear to have exercised an instant influence on no
less a personage than Madame de Sévigné, who
alludes to them certainly twice, if not oftener, and
whose great epoch of letter-writing, following upon
the marriage of Madame de Grignan, begins with
this very year, 1669. In England the influence of
the *Portuguese Letters*, as we shall presently see,
was scarcely less sudden than decisive. That we in
England needed such an influence on our letter-
writers is not to be questioned, although the faults
of English correspondence were not those of the
admirers of Voiture and Balzac. The French
needed to throw off a rhetorical insipidity ; the
English were still in the toils of the ornamental
allusiveness of the Renaissance. We find such a
sentence as the following, written by Mrs. Pen-
ruddock, in 1655, on the night before her husband's
execution, in a letter which has been preserved just
because it seemed direct, tender, and sincere :

" Those dear embraces which I yet feel and
shall never lose, being the faithful testimonies of a
loving husband, have charmed my soul to such a
reverence of your remembrance, that, were it
possible, I would, with my own blood, cement your
dead limbs to live again, and (with reverence)
think it no sin to rob Heaven a little longer of a
martyr."

Such persons as Mrs. Pénruddock never again
on such occasions as this wrote in this particular
manner, when Europe had once read the *Portuguese*

Letters. The secret of saying what was in the heart in a straightforward way was discovered, and was at once adopted by men and women a hundred times more accomplished and adroit than the Canoness of Beja.

A romantic and mysterious story had quite as much to do with the success of the *Portuguese Letters* as any directness in their style. In January 1669 a little duodecimo of 182 pages, entitled simply *Lettres Portugaises*, was issued by Barbin, the leading Paris publisher. The Letters were five in number ; they were neither signed nor addressed, and there was no indication of date or place. A prefatory note stated that they were a translation of certain Portuguese letters written to a gentleman of quality who had been serving in Portugal, and that the publisher did not know the name of the writer. He abstained from saying that he knew to whom they were addressed. Internal evidence showed that the writer was a nun in a Portuguese convent, and that she had been forsaken, after an impassioned episode, by a French cavalry officer who had loved and had ridden away. Like the hero of a Border ballad, he had passed, at the head of his regiment, through the narrow streets of the town where she lived. He had ridden not a bow-shot from her bower-eaves, and she had leaned over her balcony, for a fatal instant, and all was lost and won. The little book was read and continued to be read ; edition after edition was called for, and in 1678 the letters were stated to be written by " le Chevalier de C. . . ." Saint Simon and

Duclos each informed the world that the male personage was the Marquis of Chamilly, long afterwards Marshal of France, and a mighty warrior before the Roi-Soleil. But no indiscretion of memoir-writers gave the slightest information regarding the lady. All that appeared was that her name was Mariana and that her chamber-window looked across to the only place mentioned in the letters—Mertola, a little town on the right bank of the Guadiana. But in 1810 Boissonade, in a copy of the first edition, found a note in a contemporary hand, stating in French that the letters were written by Mariana Alcaforada, a nun in a convent at Beja, in the province of Alem-Tejo.

Beja, the theatre of the *Portuguese Letters*, is a small mediæval city, perched on a hill in the midst of the vast fertile plain of central Portugal, and boasting to this day a ring of walls and a lofty citadel, which make it a beacon from all parts of the surrounding province. What the Marquis of Chamilly was doing at Beja may now be explained, especially as, owing to the recent researches of M. Beauvois, we can for the first time follow him with some exactness. The French were in a very equivocal position with regard to Portugal. The Queen of Portugal was a French princess, and the court of Lisbon was full of Frenchmen, but Louis XIV. did not find it convenient to give Don Alfonso his open support. The fact was that Mazarin, anxious to meet the Spaniards half-way, had sacrificed Portugal in the negotiations of the Ile des Faisans. He had no intention, however, of

really leaving his old allies to the tender mercies of
Madrid, and he secretly encouraged the Portuguese
to fight for their independence. The Spaniards
had no sooner seen France sign the Treaty of the
Pyrenees, late in 1659, than they threw themselves
on the frontier of Portugal, and a guerilla war
began that lasted for nine years. All France could
openly do was to permit her own recently disbanded
foreign auxiliaries to take up service with the King
of Portugal ; and as a general for these somewhat
dubiously constituted troops, the Count of Schomberg offered peculiar advantages, as a Huguenot
and a citizen of Heidelberg. Schomberg arrived
late in 1660, and from this time forward success
leaned to the side of Portugal. M. Beauvois has
discovered that it was not until 1663 that a young
cavalry officer of great promise accompanied the
non-official envoy of France, Ablancourt, to the
court of Lisbon. This young soldier was Noël
Bouton, then known under the title of Count of St.
Léger-sur-Dheune, who had already, although only
twenty-six years of age, seen a great deal of service
in the field. He was the eleventh child of a fine
old Burgundy noble, who had trained him to arms.
In 1656 he had been taken prisoner at the siege
of Valenciennes, and had attracted the notice of
the king by a succession of gallant exploits. He is
the hero, though in a most unheroic light, of the
Portuguese Letters.

His first mission to Portugal seems to have been
diplomatic ; but on the 30th of April 1664, being
at Estremoz, on the Spanish frontier, and in the

heart of the fighting, he received from Schomberg
the command of a regiment of cavalry, and at once
took his place in the forefront of the work in hand.
His name is henceforth connected with the little
victories of this obscure and provincial war, the
results of which, none the less, were highly important to Portugal. The theatre of the campaign
was the hilly district lying between the Douro
and that part of the Guadiana which flows west-
ward before its course changes at Juramenha.
Chamilly is first mentioned with glory for his part
in the ten days' siege of Valença-de-Alcantara, in
Spain, in June 1664. A month later he helped to
defeat the Spaniards under the walls of Castello
Rodrigo, a mountain fastness in the valley of the
Douro. By this victory the independence of
Northern Portugal was secured. All through 1665
Chamilly and his dragoons hovered around Badajos,
winning laurels in June at the great battle of
Villa Viçosa ; and in October, in the flight on
Badajos, after the victory of Rio Xevora. The
war now sank to a series of marches and counter-
marches, diversified by a few skirmishes between
the Tagus and Badajos. But in September 1667,
after the Count of St. Léger, who is now Marquis
of Chamilly, has been more than three years in
Portugal, we find him for the first time distinguish-
ing himself in the plains of southern Alam-Tejo
by an attack on the Castle of Ferreira, a few miles
from Beja. It is scarcely too much to conjecture
that it was either while advancing on, or more
probably while returning from Ferreira, that he

passed under the balcony of the Franciscan convent of the Conception, and won the heart of the
susceptible canoness. So long as the war was
being prosecuted with ardour Chamilly could have
had no time for such a *liaison*, but all the troubles
of the Portuguese were practically over when
Ferreira fell. Six months later, on the 13th of
February 1668, peace was proclaimed, and Spain
accepted the independence of Portugal.[1]

A glance at the map will show the importance
of these dates and names in judging the authenticity of the letters of Mariana. Without them
the critics of those letters have been left with no
basis for conjecturing when or how, between 1661
and 1668, the Portuguese nun and the French
officer met and parted. We now see that for the
first arduous years of the campaign the young
Frenchman was not near Beja, but that he may
well have spent the last six months of his campaign-
ing in peace within or beside its walls. One or
two otherwise meaningless phrases in the letters
are now easily explicable ; and the probability

---

[1] The important sequence of facts here given with regard to
the military record of Chamilly in Portugal has never been used
before in any critical examination of the *Portuguese Letters*.
That I am able to give it is owing to the kindness of my friend
M. Jusserand, who has pointed out to me a very learned memoir
on the Chamilly family, full of fresh facts, buried by a Burgundian
historian, M. É. Beauvois, in the transactions for 1884 of a local
society, the " Société d'Histoire " of Beaune. I think I never
saw so valuable a contribution to history concealed with so
successful a modesty. I am the more anxious to express my debt
to M. Beauvois for his facts, in that I wholly disagree with his
conclusions when he comes to deal with the *Portuguese Letters*.

that the story, as tradition has sketched it for us, is mainly correct, becomes vastly greater. Before considering what these expressions are, however, it may be best to take the *Letters* themselves into our hands.

It is with some trepidation that I confess that, in my judgement, the central fact on which the chronicle of the *Portuguese Letters* hangs has hitherto been overlooked by all their editors and critics. As the *Letters* were published without dates, without indications of place or address, they took a sequence which has ever since been religiously adhered to. But reading them through very carefully—as Mark Pattison used to say all books should be read, pencil in hand—I had come to the conclusion that this order was not merely incorrect, but fatal, if persevered in, to any historic credence in the *Letters* as a whole. The fourth has all the appearance of being the earliest in date, and M. Beauvois' discoveries make this almost certain. We must understand that all the five letters are the successive appeals of a forsaken woman, who repeats her expressions of love and lamentation without much indication of scene or reason. But some such indication may, by reading the text with great care, be discovered. The fourth letter, which I believe to be the first, opens thus abruptly:

" Your lieutenant tells me that a storm forced you to put into port in the kingdom of Algarve. I am afraid that you must have greatly suffered on the sea, and this fear has so occupied me that I have thought no more about all my own troubles.

Are you quite sure that your lieutenant takes more interest than I do in all that happens to you ? Why then do you keep him better informed ? And, finally, why have you not written to me ? I am very unfortunate if you found no opportunity of writing to me before you started, and I am still more so if you did find one without using it to write to me. Your injustice and your ingratitude are extreme, yet I should be in despair if they brought you misfortune."

The tone of this is angry and indignant, but it is not the tone of a woman who considers herself abandoned. She has evidently parted with her lover unwillingly, and with suspicion, but she does not resign the right to scold him. Moreover, it is noticeable that he has but just started, and that he had hardly put to sea before he was driven into a port in Algarve. Not a critic of the *Portuguese Letters* has known what to make of this latter point, for Algarve is the strip running along the extreme south coast of Portugal, and no ship leaving Lisbon for France could possibly be driven into ports that look right across into Africa. But as we now see Chamilly slowly descending the frontier from the Douro to Beja, and as we presently find Mariana overwhelmed with emotion at the sight of the road to Mertola, we have but to look again at the map to observe that Mertola would be naturally the first stage in a journey continued south to the mouth of the Guadiana, which is navigable from that town onwards. On reaching the sea Chamilly would take ship, and would most

naturally be driven by the first storm into some
port of Algarve, from which the news would
promptly be brought back to Beja. When we find
the Portuguese nun speaking of some early con-
fidences as made " five or six months ago," and
when we recollect that the capture of Ferreira
took place five months before the peace with
Spain, we can hardly doubt that the events upon
which the *Letters* are founded took place between
September 1667 and February 1668, soon after
which latter date Chamilly doubtless made an
excuse for setting forth for France. Thus a series
of minute expressions in this so-called fourth letter
—expressions hitherto meaningless or misleading
—are shown to be of vital importance in testifying
to the genuineness of the correspondence.

Another fragment from this same letter will
help to complete the picture of Chamilly's de-
sertion :

" You have taken advantage of the excuses
which you had for going back to France. A ship
was starting. Why did you not let her start ?
Your family had written to you. Do you not
know what persecutions I have endured from
mine ? Your honour compelled you to forsake
me. Have I been so solicitous about my honour ?
You were forced to go to serve your king. If all
that is said of him be true, he has no need of your
help, and he would have excused you. I should
have been only too happy had we passed our lives
together ; but since a cruel absence had to divide
us, it seems to me that I ought to be satisfied in

knowing that I am not faithless to you. Indeed, for all the world contains would I not commit so base an action. What! have you known the depths of my heart and my affection, and have yet been able to persuade yourself to abandon me for ever, and to expose me to the terror of believing that you will for the future only think of me to sacrifice the memory of me to some new passion!"

The freedom with which this cloistered lady and her foreign lover met has been objected to as improbable. But the manners of Portugal in the seventeenth century gave to women of the religious orders a social freedom denied to ordinary wives and daughters. In the *Mémoires* of Ablancourt, whom Chamilly attended on his first mission to Lisbon, we read of royal parties of pleasure at the Convent of Santa Speranza, where the nuns and courtiers mingled in theatrical representations before the king and queen. Another contemporary account admits that the French and English were so much beloved in Portugal that some liberty was allowed to them beyond what a Portuguese gentleman might indulge in. It is easy to see that if convents might without scandal be opened to men in social intercourse, it is not probable that they would be closed to a brilliant foreign ally fresh from Villa Viçosa or Ferreira. But we must again allow Mariana Alcaforada to tell her own tale :

"Everyone has noticed the entire change in my mood, my manners, and my person. My mother has spoken to me about it, with bitterness at first,

and then with a certain kindliness. I do not know
what I said to her in reply ; I fancy I must have
confessed everything to her. The strictest of the
nuns here are sorry to see what a condition I am
in ; they even treat me on account of it with some
consideration and some tenderness. Everybody
is touched at my love, and you alone remain
perfectly indifferent, writing me only cold letters,
full of repetitions ; half the paper is not filled, and
you are rude enough to let me see that you are
dying with impatience to be done writing. Doña
Brites has been persecuting me these last days to
get me to leave my room ; and fancying that it
would amuse me, she took me for a turn on the
balcony from which one has a view of Mertola ; I
went with her, and at once a cruel memory came
back to me, a memory which kept me weeping all
the remainder of the day. She brought me back,
and I threw myself on my bed, where I could but
reflect a thousand times over how little chance there
was of my ever being cured. Whatever is done to
solace me augments my suffering, and in the
remedies themselves I find intimate reasons why
I should be wretched. I have often seen you pass
that spot with an air that charmed me, and I was
on that balcony on that fatal day when I first
began to feel the symptoms of my ill-starred passion.
I fancied that you wished to please me, although
you did not know me. I persuaded myself that
you had noticed me among all the ladies that were
with me. I imagined that when you drew rein,
you were well pleased that I should have a better

sight of you, and that I should admire your skill and how graceful you looked on horseback. I was surprised to notice that I was frightened when you took your horse through a difficult place ; the fact is that I was taking a secret interest in all your actions."

We see that he wrote to her at first, although not from that port of Algarve, in which he had thought of nothing but business. It does not appear that after this he ever wrote again, nor as her memory loses its sharpness does she ever, after this first letter, regain the same clearness of reminiscence. We may quote once more from this, the most interesting of the famous five. It is thus that Mariana closes her pathetic appeal :

" I want to have the portraits of your brother and of your sister-in-law. Whatever is anything to you is very dear to me, and I am wholly devoted to what concerns you. I have no will of my own left. There are moments in which it seems to me that I should be humble enough to serve her whom you love. . . . An officer has been waiting for this letter for a long time ; I had made up my mind to write it in such a way that you may not be disgusted when you receive it, but I see I have made it too extravagant. I must close it. Alas ! it is out of my power to do so. I seem to be talking to you when I write to you, and you become a little more present to me then. . . . The officer who is to take this letter reminds me for the fourth time that he wishes to start. What a hurry he is in ! He, no doubt, is forsaking some unhappy lady in this country. Farewell! it is harder for me to finish my letter than it was for you to abandon me, perhaps for ever."

The remaining letters give fewer indications of date and sequence than the fourth, nor are they so picturesque. But the reader will not seek the *Portuguese Letters*, as he seeks the *Mémoires* of Madame de Motteville, or even the correspondence of Madame de Sévigné, mainly for sparkling incident and the pretty details of contemporary life. The value of these epistles rests in their sincerity as a revelation of the heart. Poor Mariana had no inclination to describe the daily life of her fellow-nuns or the intrigues of society in Beja. She has been deceived, the man she loves is absent, and as she weeps without cessation, she cannot help confessing to herself that she does not expect to see him back again.

" I resigned my life to you," she says in the so-called first letter, " as soon as I saw you, and I feel some pleasure now in sacrificing to you what you will not accept. A thousand times a day I send my sighs out after you ; they search for you everywhere, and for all reward of so much disquietude what do they bring me back but too sincere a warning from my evil fortune, which is too cruel to suffer me to deceive myself, and which says to me every moment, Cease, cease, unfortunate Mariana ! vainly thou dost consume thyself, vainly dost seek a lover whom thou shalt never see again, who has crost the ocean to escape from thee, who is now in France in the midst of pleasures, who gives no single moment to the thought of thy sufferings, and who can well dispense with all these thy needless transports."

She will not, however, yet admit that she is wholly deserted. She has received a letter from him, and though its tone was so far from responding to her own that it threw her beside herself for three hours, it has reawakened her hopes.

" Can you ever be contented by a passion less ardent than mine ? You will, perhaps, find elsewhere more beauty (although you used to tell me that I was beautiful enough), but you will never find so much love again, and all the rest is nothing. Do not fill out your letters with needless matter, and you may save yourself the trouble of reminding me to remember you. I cannot forget you, and I cannot forget, too, that you made me hope that you would come back to me for awhile. Ah ! why will you not spend all your life here ? Were it possible for me to quit this wretched cloister, I would not stay in Portugal to see whether you performed your promises. I would not count the cost, but would fly to seek you, to follow you, to love you. I dare not persuade myself that this will be ; I will not nourish such a hope (though there might be pleasure in delusion), for since I am doomed to be unhappy, I will have no feelings inconsistent with my lot."

The violent and wretched tone of the *Letters* culminates in the third, which is unsurpassed as a revelation of the ingenious self-torture of a sensitive mind brooding upon its own despair. The women

of Paris were astonished to read such pages as the
following, where complex emotions which they had
often experienced or imagined, but had never been
able to formulate, suddenly found perfectly direct
and limpid expression :

" I cannot persuade myself to wish that you
may no longer be thinking about me ; and, indeed,
to speak sincerely, I am furiously jealous of whatever may give you happiness, and of all that may
touch your heart and your tastes in France. I do
not know why I write to you. I see well enough
that you will only pity me, and I do not wish for
your pity. I am very angry with myself when I
reflect upon all that I have sacrificed for you. I
have exposed myself to the rage of my relatives,
to the severity of the laws of this country against
nuns, and to your ingratitude, which appears to
me the greatest of all misfortunes. Yet, all the
while, I am conscious that my remorse is not
sincere, and that for the love of you I would with
all my heart run into far greater dangers than any
of these."

The extraordinary and at that time the unique
merit of the Portuguese Nun, as a letter-writer, lies
in the fact that, in the full tempest and turmoil of
her passion, she never yields to the temptation
of giving herself up to rhetoric, or rather that
whenever she does make a momentary concession
to this habit of her age, she doubles on herself
immediately, and is the first to deprecate such false
flowers of speech. She knows that her letters are
too long, although she cannot keep them within

bounds. It is part of the torture of her spirit that she recognises better than any monitor from without could teach her, that her lamentations, reproaches, and entreaties are as little calculated as a material flood of tears would be to revive the fire upon the hearth of sunken embers. As she clamours at the door of memory, and makes the air resound with her importunity, she is sane enough to be aware all the while that these are no seductions by which a weary heart may be refreshed and re-awakened ; yet is she absolutely powerless to moderate her own emotion. The result is poignant to the last degree ; and from the absence of all, or almost all, surrounding local colour of incident or tradition, the spectacle of this distress removes and excites the reader in somewhat the same fashion as the loud crying of an unseen figure out-of-doors in the darkness of the night may move the helpless sympathy of one who listens from a window.

Nothing more is known of this shadowy Mariana Alcaforada, but the author of her misfortunes figures long and gloriously in French history. His fatuity, if not his heartlessness, in allowing her letters to be immediately printed, is a blot upon his humanity in our eyes, but seems to have abated his magnificence not a whit among his contemporaries. It would be idle to inquire by what means the letters came into the hands of a publisher. In 1690, upon the death of the translator, it was admitted that they had been turned out of Portuguese into excellent French by

A NUN'S LOVE LETTERS

Pierre Girardin de Guilleragues, a "Gascon gourmand," as Saint-Simon calls him, immortalised moreover by Boileau, in a graceful couplet, as being—

> Born master of all arts a court can teach,
> And skilled alike in silence and in speech.

It was Guilleragues who said of Pelisson that " he abused the permission that men have to be ugly." He was patronised by Madame de Maintenon and died French ambassador to the Porte in 1689. To Guilleragues is attributed the composition of the *Portuguese Letters* by those who seek to deny that Mariana Alcaforada ever existed. But in their own day no one doubted that the actors in this little drama were real persons. Chamilly is described by Saint-Simon as a tall, heavy man, extremely good-natured and gallant in fight, although to listen to and to look at, giving little suggestion that he could ever have inspired so romantic a passion as that revealed by the *Portuguese Letters*. To this there is an obvious reply, that Saint-Simon only knew Chamilly in his mature years, and that there is no reason why a heavy dragoon should not have been very attractive to a Portuguese maiden at twenty-six and yet seem most unattractive at forty-six to the wittiest of memoir-writers. To the Portuguese nun he undoubtedly behaved disgracefully ill, and not at all like a Christian gentleman ; but we must remember that his own age judged such bad deeds as peccadillos in the free campaign of love and

151

war. Chamilly's subsequent career was unquestionably glorious. He fought the Turks in
Candia, he commanded the troops of the Electors
of Cologne and of Munster, he won deathless
laurels at the famous siege of Grave ; and, finally,
after twenty-five campaigns, he ended as Marshal
of France, and married a wife who was, as we
may smile maliciously to read in our Saint-Simon,
" singularly ugly."

The success of the *Portuguese Letters* was
attested not merely by the multitude of successive
editions of the text, but by the imitations and
continuations which were foisted upon a credulous
public. Only seven months after the original
publication there appeared a second part containing seven letters, with the same date, 1669, on
the title-page. These did not, however, pretend
to be written by Mariana, but by a Portuguese
lady of quality. The style was very different, as
the publisher admitted, and the letters bear every
stamp of artifice and fiction. They were, however, greedily accepted as genuine, and the
" Dame Portugaise " took her place beside the
" Religieuse." The temptation to prolong the
romance was irresistible, and there was immediately published a pamphlet of " Replies," five in
number, supposed to be sent by the French officer
to the Portuguese nun in answer to each of her
letters. This came from a Parisian press ; but the
idea of publishing the officer's letters had occurred
simultaneously to a provincial bookseller, and still
in the same year, 1669, there appeared at Grenoble

a volume of *New Replies*, six in number, the first
being not properly a reply, but an introductory
letter. This last publication openly professes to
be fiction. The editor states in the preface that
being " neither a girl, nor a nun, nor even perhaps
in love," he cannot pretend to express the
sentiments of the heart with the genuine vigour of
the original letters ; but that, as Aulus Sabinus
ventured to reply to certain of the heroic epistles
of Ovid, though with so little success as merely
to heighten the lustre of those originals, so he
hopes by these inventions, and a mere *jeu d'esprit*,
to increase the admiration of readers for Mariana's
genuine correspondence. All this is very honest
and very legitimate, but so eager were the ladies
of the seventeenth century to be deluded that this
preface of the guileless editor was taken to be a
mere mystification, and the Grenoble *New Replies*
were swallowed like the rest. Some idea of the
popularity of the *Portuguese Letters* may be gained,
not merely from the vogue of these successive
imitations, but from the fact that M. Eugène Asse,
the latest and best of Mariana's editors, has
described no fewer than sixteen editions of the
Letters themselves, issued before the close of the
seventeenth century, a list which would seem to
be very far indeed from being complete.

Rousseau was the first to start the idea that the
Portuguese Letters were written by a man. He
went upon no external evidence, but on subtle and
in truth very fanciful arguments regarding the
point of view taken by the writer. No one else has

seriously questioned their authenticity, until quite recently, when M. Beauvois, a Burgundian antiquary, has endeavoured to destroy our faith in the existence of the Portuguese nun. This gentleman is an impassioned admirer of the exploits of the Marquis of Chamilly, and it is not difficult to perceive that his wish to discredit the *Letters* is due to his desire to whitewash the character of his hero, blackened for the present, at all events to modern eyes, by the cruel abandonment of this poor religious lady in the Beja convent. This critic goes on to the opposite extreme, and allows himself to speak of Máriana's letters as "the obsessions of a Mænad." Many of M. Beauvois's acute objections are met by the rearrangement of the letters which I have suggested above, and particularly by the fact that the fourth of them should certainly stand the first. After a careful examination of his criticism, and particularly in the light of the important historical dates, with regard to Chamilly's record in the Portuguese war, which M. Beauvois has himself brought forward, I for one am more persuaded than ever that the outline of the story as we know it is true, and that the letters, or something Portuguese which was very like them, were actually sent after the rascally *bellâtre* when he made his way back to France in 1668.

Bare as the letters are, there are nevertheless little touches of detail here and there, little inexplicable allusions, such as a real correspondence would possess, and such as no forger would intro-

duce. It would be tedious in this place to dwell
minutely on this sort of evidence, but a single
example may be given. In one passage the nun
writes, "Ah! how I envy the happiness of
Emmanuel and of Francisque. Why am not I
always with you, as they are!" Nothing more
is said of these beings. We are left to conjecture
whether they were fellow-officers, or servants, or
dogs, or even perhaps parrots. A forger would
scarcely leave two meaningless names in the body
of his text without some indication of his idea.
The sincerity, moreover, of the style and sentiments is extraordinary, and is observed to great
advantage by comparing the various continuations
and replies with the five original letters. To
suppose the first little volume of 1669 to be a
deliberate fiction would be to land us in the more
serious difficulty of discovering in its inventor a
great imaginative creator of emotional romance.
The hero-worship of M. Beauvois has not convinced me that Mariana never gazed across the
olives and oranges to Mertola, nor watched the
cavalcade of her false dragoon file down into the
gorge of the Guadiana.

The French critics have not taken any interest
in the influence of the *Portuguese Letters* in
England. Yet translations and imitations of
these letters became very numerous in this country
before the close of the seventeenth century. The
earliest version which I have been able to trace is
that of Sir Roger L'Estrange, published as a very
tiny little book of *Five Love-Letters from a Nun*

to a Cavalier, in 1678 (December 28, 1677). In a
short preface to the reader, the translator says,
" These five letters are here at your service. You
will find in them the lively image of an extravagant
and an unfortunate passion, and that a woman
may be flesh and blood in a cloister as well as
in a palace." This translation of L'Estrange's
went on being reprinted for fifty years, and was
attended on its successful course from one toilet
to another by a variety of imitations, the liveliest
of which is attributed to the pen of the vivacious
Major Richardson Pack. From the first the
Portuguese Letters were not presented to the
women of England as literature, but as models
of sincere letter-writing, and hence they escaped
mention in our solemn handbooks of bibliography
and literary history. But their influence was
extraordinary, and by the time that the *Spectator*
had come into existence, and Richard Steele was
sitting over his wine, " the slave of beauty,"
writing out of his heart to Mary Scurlock, the men
and women of England had learned the lesson
which the nun of Beja was betrayed to teach them,
and they could say in plain, straightforward sentences exactly what it was in their souls to express
to one another, without any sort of trope or
rhetorical ornament.

THE FAIRY IN THE GARDEN

THE FAIRY IN THE GARDEN

OF all English poets now on the happy side of fifty, it is Mr. Walter de la Mare who has had the most direct influence on the writers of his own day. This is the more remarkable because it has been gained by no expenditure of advertising energy, or even by the exercise of any faculty not directly dependent on poetry. No living author is more hidden from the public view than Mr. de la Mare, nor is there one who contributes less to the discussion of themes of general interest. In the loud chorus of those who desire to improve us, and change us, and set our heels where our heads used to be, he is obstinately silent. He puts forward no theories, starts no heresies, and leads no troop to battle. If it were possible to overlook Mr. de la Mare he would remain invisible, and if he is perceived it is precisely as a violet is betrayed by its perfume.

He is revealed by the penetrating intensity of his genius, and not by any effort of his own to obtain notice or to arrest attention. As a poet he is a creation of the twentieth century, and he started the rich harvest of the " Georgians," as it is the fashion to call them. He is the quietest and the least obtrusive of them all, but by dint of his consistency and his pertinacious fidelity to one definite type of beauty, he continues to lead them.

His delicate, cool music runs in an undertone at the root of everything that is produced in serious verse to-day, and yet nothing is more difficult than to define the character of his art.

When Mr. Walter de la Mare began to write, twenty years ago, the prestige of the latest Victorians was but faintly questioned. I refuse to consider that it is questioned now, in any reasonable court of judgement, but there is a great difference between an historical appreciation of merit and a belief that in Tennyson picturesque description had said its last word, that no philosophical poetry would supersede Browning, or that in Swinburne verse had reached its limit of precision and beauty. The real heresy about the Victorians lay not in recognising their power and skill, but in supposing that they had exhausted Nature, and that no writers would, even in the future, do more than fumble along the path where Meredith and Arnold had climbed with springing footsteps.

Mr. Walter de la Mare's earliest volume, called *Songs of Childhood*, did not attract much attention, partly because of its quietness, but more because it was entirely out of key with the poetry fashionable at the end of the nineteenth century. In ethical respects extremely unlike the verse of Mr. Thomas Hardy, that of Mr. de la Mare, especially in its earlier manifestations, has this in common with it, that it examines with scrupulous care little phenomena of Nature, and of Nature acting upon the soul, which had appeared too insignificant to attract the attention of other recent

poets. But the *Songs of Childhood* also exemplified
a quality which is essential to Mr. de la Mare, the
delicate splendour of his fancy, as in " Tartary "
and in " The Isle of Lone," exhibited often with
a recklessness which is on the border of incoherency, but is preserved by a happy instinct from
passing outside the bounds of what poetry permits
itself. The authors of past time with whom Mr.
de la Mare has most in common are Blake (in the
Songs of Innocence), Coleridge (in *Kubla Khan*),
and Christina Rossetti (in *Goblin Market*). He
has not borrowed from these magicians, but his
enchantments are of the same order as theirs.

All Mr. de la Mare's poems are short, and many
of them are epigrams, in the Greek sense, mere
seed-pearls of song. Very rarely he exceeds the
limit of forty lines, and when he is tempted to do
so he is not always at his happiest. It seems as
though a brief flight of music suited best the interpretation of the fugitive moods and aery visions
which sweep over his spirit. Perhaps the central
feature of his poetry is the place which beauty
takes in the expression of it. Life is a dream to
him, but it is not, as it is to so many writers nowadays, a slumber haunted by hideous and loathsome
images, but a serene region in which wonder and
mystery have not destroyed, but have a little dis-
arranged the common and logical sequence of
experience. The poet is passive under the stress
of the illusions which pass before his eyes between
sleeping and waking, and a beauty which is
beyond all earthly compass continually floats

across him, masking the realities of earth. It is especially in fragrant gardens that his vision reveals to him the mystery and the wonder of the world :

> Speak not—whisper not ;
> Here bloweth thyme and bergamot ;
> Softly on the evening hour,
> Secret herbs their spices shower.
> Dark-spiked rosemary and myrrh,
> Lean-stalked, purple lavender ;
> Hides within her bosom, too,
> All her sorrows, bitter rue.

The last of these couplets exemplifies a certain weakness of structure in Mr. de la Mare's verse. What he means to say is that " bitter rue, also, hides all her sorrows within her bosom," but he disperses the words in defiance of their ordinary sequence. This seems to arise out of a certain languor characteristic of his mind, but it is to be noticed, also, that when the ear is accustomed to these inversions and contortions they cease to offer any discomfort.

In " The Children of Stare," which seems to be the earliest fully characteristic poem of Mr. de la Mare, we find already present the main qualities of his verse, its note of twilight reverie, its touch of bright colour, its Æolian melody rising and falling. This piece is worthy of close attention ; it exemplifies the essential character of the writer. We are introduced to a winter scene in the garden of an ancient house where everything would be silent and sinister but for the presence of children whose

" small and heightened faces " are " like wine-red winter buds." In six stanzas we have a finished picture of the group, in gay dresses, playing against the wintry background, faintly glittering in the moon ; it is like some Dutch water-colour drawing of the seventeenth century. And, very suggestively, this icy merriment in the dim light fills the poet's heart not with commonplace reflections appropriate to the scene, but with strange emotions, " thick mystery, wild peril, law like an iron rod."

The power of fear is never far out of the range of Mr. de la Mare's vision. He expatiates on the horror of little noises heard at night, while the deluding echoes of birds calling in the sky stir him with vague apprehension. The world for him is full of intimidating whispers and phantom footfalls, and when darkness falls upon the garden he shivers at bodiless presences which pass him and repass. In all this he is like a child, incident to fears, as Shakespeare puts it, unaffected by argument or proof, but ready at a moment's notice to create around himself a world of mystery and panic.

The art of expressing the inexpressible has been given to Mr. de la Mare in rare fullness. If a central feature of his poetry is its tranquillity, it is not quiet with self-satisfaction or aplomb ; but hushed as one who hangs on tiptoe to hear a rustling sound, or to watch a furtive shadow in the woodland. An examination of one of his poems will throw light on his method in nearly all of them, and I therefore quote the whole of " The Mocking Fairy " :

" Won't you look out of your window, Mrs. Gill? "
  Quoth the Fairy, nidding, nodding in the garden
" *Can't* you look out of your window, Mrs. Gill? "
  Quoth the Fairy, laughing softly in the garden ;
But the air was still, the cherry boughs were still,
And the ivy-tod 'neath the empty sill,
And never from her window looked out Mrs. Gill
  On the Fairy shrilly mocking in the garden.

" What have they done with you, poor Mrs. Gill? "
  Quoth the Fairy, brightly dancing in the garden ;
" Where have they hidden you, you poor old Mrs. Gill? "
  Quoth the Fairy, brightly glancing in the garden ;
But night's faint veil now wrapped the hill,
Stark 'neath the stars stood the dead-still mill,
And out of her cold cottage never answered Mrs. Gill
  The Fairy mimbling-mambling in the garden.

This little poem, like all the dominant class in Mr. de la Mare's work, produces the impression of a thing seen at twilight, from a certain distance, by a near-sighted person. Nothing is plainly distinguished, but a series of indefinite yet intelligible touches give a mysterious and highly imaginative result. What are the relations of Mrs. Gill and the Fairy? What " have they done " with poor Mrs. Gill? Is she dead, or merely dull and indifferent? Is the Fairy beneficent or sinister, a friendly or merely a taunting spirit? We do not know, and the answer to these questions is completely immaterial, because it is not the poet's aim to tell a clear tale, but to awaken in us emotions of fear, wonder, and faint pity. What is not immaterial is to note that in producing these shadowy effects the poet does not fall back upon carelessness of diction.

On the contrary, it is when his pictures are most phantasmal, and the moods he presents most elusive, that his language becomes peculiarly choice. Consider the fastidious appropriateness of every epithet in the lyric called " Winter," of every selected tone in the little harmony called " The Song of the Secret."

It is not only in the tenebrous and the phantasmal that Mr. de la Mare excels. He has also a mood in which he indulges in sunlit images and a profusion of colour. These are the moments in which he is " crazed with the spell " of Arabian vision, and the world is shining for him in sunbeams and dew. But the essential character is the same, and the outlook upon life is still the unreasoning impression of childhood. Very characteristic is the ballad I have already mentioned, " The Isle of Lone," one of the most elaborate which the author has published. What would the rough Scotch critics, the Jeffreys who hooted to Wordsworth, " This will never do ! " who swept Keats back to his " gallipots," have said to this preposterous tale of three dwarfs who lived alone in a tropic island in the company of apes and parrots ?

> They sate to sup in a jasmine bower
>   Lit pale with flies of fire,
> Their bowls the hue of the iris-flower,
>   And lemon their attire.

They taught three old apes to sing, they fished and they hunted foxes, they blew music out of twisted shells, and they raced with their night-caps on

through the surf of the dark-green sea. But at
last two of them quarrelled, and drowned one
another, while the survivor transferred the night-
caps to the apes, and then expired in a coral grot.
This is the instance in which Mr. de la Mare has
resigned himself most unreservedly to the illogical
dream of childhood. The result is saved from
failure by its beauty, but we approach the confines
of absurdity. " Off the Ground," in which the
three farmers dance down to the sea, has the same
character, perhaps more legitimately exercised.

The gift of Mr. de la Mare is confined within a
small circle, and he has to beware of repeating his
effects too constantly. If it were necessary to hint
a fault in his poetry it would be a certain tendency
to monotony. It is therefore better to dwell on a
few of his lyrics at a time than to attempt to read
them all. Three or four of his songs and ballads,
chosen from any section of his books, reveal his
extreme and sensitive delicacy, his tranquillity of
imagination, his purity and elegance. He is the
type of the romantic lyrist, delivered from all bonds
of logic and definition. His humble genius knows
no touch of arrogance or disdain. It wanders up
and down the woodland brooks exhaling its " in-
flexible douceur " (as Anatole France might say)
in a music sweeter than their own.

THE OXFORD SAUSAGE

THE OXFORD SAUSAGE

PICKED up on a suburban bookstall, a little volume, annoying me at first by what seemed its impenetrable reserve, ended by exciting my curiosity to the last degree. *The Oxford Sausage* bears no editor's name, its anonymous preface is designed to mislead, and its contents show no evidence of design. It is a collection of facetious copies of verse, illustrating university life, and its title-page claims that all of them are witty, *tota*, *merum sal*. *Tota* is going too far, but many of the poems are funny, and all are unfamiliar. But they cannot have been highly familiar even to readers of this reprint of 1815, since the Oxford they illustrate was the Oxford of more than half a century earlier than that.

The Oxford Sausage, as I will presently explain, emanated from Trinity; in the following year, 1816, a graceful youth named John Henry Newman matriculated at that college. The contrast between old and new could not be made more emphatic. The first discovery about the *Sausage* is that it was, in 1815, a reprint; the original having appeared, with a like furtiveness, in 1764. Half a century had made a great difference in social manners, yet there is no change, or very little, in the verses. In order that I might reduce and recognise the allusions, I called to my aid a powerful ally in my learned friend, Dr. William Hunt, who responded with zealous generosity. It is due to Dr. Hunt's help that I am able to give some account of an amusing and, as it seems, entirely forgotten volume. Anthologies are in the fashion to-day. Here is one which was popular in the Universities (for Cambridge had her share) in the days of Dr. Johnson.

The carefully concealed editor of *The Oxford Sausage* was a man famous in his day and by no means forgotten now, Dr. Thomas Warton. He was the author of the earliest and long the best *History of English Poetry*, he was a poet himself and in his day a metrical innovator, but he was above all an Oxford man. His whole life was spent in the odour which breathes around *The Oxford Sausage*, an atmosphere of strong tobacco and foaming ale, Latin quotations, and endless conversation. By 1764 Warton was already a Fellow of Trinity College and Professor of Poetry, as well as the author of many serious works ; so that he might well not be anxious to appear as the compiler of a book of local songs, all frivolous, and some not decent. So he wrote a preface, warning readers not to try to discover who the editor was, and especially not to suppose him to be the author of the anonymous *Companion to the Guide to Oxford* and of *Terræ Filius*, because " most unluckily the author of those pieces will never be known."

This was very sly, because these were not the same person, *Terræ Filius* being the work of a rapscallion called Nicholas Amhurst, long dead by 1764; and the *Companion* — oh! what a deceitful professor — being written by Warton himself! He slipped into the *Sausage* several poems of his own, of course without his name. Dr. Hunt has identified some of them for me, but there is one, the satire called "Newmarket," which there could be no mystery about, since Warton had openly published it thirteen years earlier. I wish that Dr. Hunt could find it in his heart to turn for an hour from sterner investigations and publish an annotated edition of *The Oxford Sausage*. No book is in more need of editing, and no one more capable of fulfilling such a task than the late President of the Royal Historical Society.

The exposure of university life which Gibbon makes in his *Autobiography* has often been quoted, and has been charged with exaggeration. "The Fellows or monks of my time were decent, easy men who supinely enjoyed the gifts of the founder. . . . From the toil of reading, writing, or thinking they had absolved their consciences." The verses in *The Oxford Sausage*, whether satirical, Bacchanalian, or merely frivolous, confirm the judgement of Gibbon. Here is part of a picture of "the peaceful Fellows," probably from the pen of Warton himself:

> No chattering females crowd their social fire,
> No dread have they of discord and of strife,
> Unknown the names of Husband and of Sire,
> Unfelt the plagues of matrimonial life.

Oft have they basked along the sunny walls ;
  Oft have the benches bowed beneath their weight ;
How jocund are their looks when dinner calls !
How smoke their cutlets on the crowded plate !

O, let not Temperance too disdainful hear
  How long our Feasts, how long our Dinners last ;
Nor let the Fair with a contemptuous sneer
  On these unmarried men reflections cast !

Historians, such as Mr. Christopher Wordsworth, confirm the impression which these verses give. In the generation previous to *The Oxford Sausage*, the University, strongly Jacobite and disloyal to the House of Hanover, had been kept from stagnation by its political anxieties. But after 1745 slumber fell on Oxford. Professors were silent, college tutors grew inefficient, discipline was relaxed. The first Lord Malmesbury, writing of the very year when the *Sausage* appeared, describes the utter looseness of rule. Undergraduates could absent themselves when they pleased, and go off to town. His own tutor, " a worthy man," did not " concern himself with his pupils." This is the tone revealed throughout the verses of *The Oxford Sausage*.

But Thomas Warton himself was far removed from the lazy type of the college don, who

    to thoughtless ignorance a prey,
Neglects to hold short dalliance with a book.

He was full of intellectual curiosity and creative energy. Nevertheless, the stamp of the Oxford of 1750 was upon him. In the common-room of

THE OXFORD SAUSAGE

Trinity College, where through so many evenings he drank beer and smoked a churchwarden, flung his grizzle wig over the back of his chair, and discoursed on black-letter folios and the versification of Chaucer, there hangs to this day his admirable portrait painted by Sir Joshua Reynolds.

When Warton was brought to Streatham to be presented to Fanny Burney, that stringent judge of men pronounced him " unformed in his manners and awkward in his gestures. He joined not one word in the general talk." No doubt, the elegant author of *Evelina* was not of the world of Tom Warton, who was unaccustomed to the society of females; yet when he got back to Trinity, he would once more become the life and soul of the common-room. There he talked with wit and copiousness, though unfortunately in a voice which was said to be like the gobble of a turkey-cock. He was a privileged enthusiast, who was known to have once, at least, ventured on wearing a crown of laurel. His heavy body was not prone to violent exercise, but he was fond of walking along the river, with a pipe in his mouth, while he chatted with the watermen. We may think of him so, or trying to rouse enthusiasm by lecturing in Latin to a languid class of students. Either way, he was the antithesis of the typical college don of the period, and the idle, guzzling University which he mocked and loved is mirrored in his *Oxford Sausage*.

Good-natured in the extreme, Warton shows his easy temper by printing in *The Oxford Sausage* a

skit upon himself ; or, perhaps, was that a blind
—who knows ? Michael Wodhull, of Brasenose,
was the author of the " Ode to Criticism," which
ridicules " The Triumph of Isis," a serious poem
which Warton had published in 1749. But Wodhull was a famous book-collector, whose library
contained black - letter treasures which Warton
may have been anxious to consult. He is not
so kind to all contemporary antiquaries, since a
parody of the ballad of " Chevy Chase " pokes fun
at Browne Willis, whose books about the English
cathedrals are still of value. Faded shadows,
most of the famous figures in this book, but I
should like to know more about Herbert Beaver,
who is not in the *Dictionary of National Biography.*
He is the author here of " The Cushion Plot," a
very vivacious ballad, recounting the adventures
of Dr. Shaw, head of " Teddy " Hall, who was
called " Gaby " :

> When Gaby possession had got of the Hall,
> He took a survey of the Chapel and all,
> Since that, like the rest, was just ready to fall,
> > Which nobody can deny.
>
> And first he began to examine the chest,
> Where he found an old cushion which gave him distaste,
> The first of the kind that e'er troubled his rest,
> > Which nobody can deny,

this cushion having embroidered on it, in letters
of gold, a device which might be either Jacobite
or Georgian. Dr. Hunt has found out that Beaver,
who was Superior Beadle at Law to the University,

had a public scuffle with one Yeats, which occupied
the idle attention of Oxford. Here was a subject
for a ballad of which *The Oxford Sausage* failed
to take advantage. It is difficult to account for a
footnote which speaks of St. Edmund's Hall as a
" College," and its Principal as the " President."
A foreigner making this double blunder would be
withered by Oxonian sarcasm.

Light is thrown by various poems in the *Sausage*
on the relaxations of University life. The gentlemen commoners, being men of fashion, affected
riding, horse-racing, and driving. On Sundays
they rode

> With hat new-cock'd, and newly laced,
> O'er mutton-chops and scanty wine
> At humble Dorchester to dine.

Cock-fighting in the pit in Holywell had been
forbidden by the Vice-Chancellor, but was winked
at elsewhere. There was some tennis for the richer
and some billiards for the poorer men, but very
little. Undergraduates, scarcely more than boys
in those days, amused themselves with walks,
skittles, and quoits. There is here a mention of
rowing for pleasure :

> No more the wherry feels my stroke so true ;
> At skittles in a grizzle can I play ?
> Woodstock, farewell ! and Wallingford adieu !
> Where many a scheme relieved the lingering day,

sighs the scholar promoted to the immobility of a
Fellowship. The exercise of the skittle-yard was
looked upon with favour by the college authorities

as encouraging a game " founded on arithmetical and geometrical principles." The absence of any mention of cricket or football will be noted. I think that neither of these games was played at all prominently in Oxford during the eighteenth century ; to Cambridge I fancy that lads coming up from Eton may have brought a certain amount of school tradition with them, but not to Oxford. Every year, from 1754, at least, there was circulated through the University by the bellman a copy of rhymes called *The Oxford Newsman's Verses*. These were occupied with every description of local tittle-tattle, but there occurs in them not a word about those amusements which now absorb undergraduate attention.

The editor of *The Oxford Sausage* was but thirty-six years of age, but his ways were already settled, and it is notable that he consistently looks backward and not forward. He would not have sympathised with Lord Haldane's call to the heights, nor is there the slightest hint that he saw around him any revival of enthusiasm or earnestness. Warton had plenty of humanism, but it was not in the least idealistic, and in this respect he was abreast of his time and not a step in front of it. But he looked back with veneration on the isolated scholars who had preserved Oxford from reproach in the previous generation, and particularly on the wonderful and isolated figure of Thomas Hearne, the *architypographus* to the University, whom Warton can scarcely have known in person, since Hearne died, in his rooms in

college, in 1735, when Warton was a child. The
"Epistle" from Hearne is doubtless a mystification ; in it the spirit of the great persecuted antiquary sarcastically congratulates Warton on the
disfavour now shown by the Oxford fellows to
every kind of research. I fail to grasp the allusion
in the lines :

> Cruel as the mandate
> Of mitred priests, who Baskett late enjoined
> To throw aside the reverend letters black,
> And print Fast Prayers in modern type.

But it is part of a lamentation appropriately put
in the mouth of Hearne, who, though no house in
Oxford " had so rich a furniture " in his eyes as
the Bodleian, was not merely dismissed from his
post there as a punishment for his non-juring
convictions, but was positively forbidden in the
midst of his unrivalled investigations, to enter the
Library. This was a shameful piece of tyranny.
I find little reference in *The Oxford Sausage* to
discord between Whigs and Jacobites, doubtless
because after 1760 the Jacobite question ceased to
be a burning one, though it is neatly summed up
in Beaver's ballad of "The Cushion Plot," to which
I have already referred.

From a "Panegyric on Oxford Ale," which I am
disposed to attribute to the pen of Thomas Warton
himself, I take a passage characteristic of English
versification in 1764, modified as it had become
by the influence of Thomson and Young, and
equally descriptive of the duller side of college
life :

All powerful ALE ! Thy sorrow-soothing sweets
Oft I repeat in vacant afternoon,
When tatter'd stockings crave my mending hand
Not unexperienced ; while the tedious toil
Slides unregarded. Let the tender swain
Each morn regale on nerve-relaxing Tea,
Companion meet of languor-loving nymph :
Be mine each morn, with eager appetite
And hunger undissembled, to repair
To friendly Buttery ; there on smoking crust
And foaming Ale to banquet unrestrained,
Material breakfast !

Tea, at about a shilling an ounce, was still a luxury, not to be wasted on a serious meal like breakfast, but to be reserved for some special occasion when, as *Terræ Filius* tells us, the scholar had the privilege of sipping it, " after Prayers, with some celebrated toast."

BURLESQUE

BURLESQUE

BURLESQUE is a little province of English literature which historians have neglected, and, I think, misunderstood. It enjoyed a sudden development and brief vogue in the middle of the seventeenth century, and to this we may devote a little attention. First of all, we may turn to the encyclopaedias for the broader aspect, and they inform us that the name comes from the Italian, *burla*, a joke ; that the ancients practised the thing, especially in the Homeric *Battle of the Frogs and Mice* ; and that the Italian epic poet Berni excelled in travesty.

But all this, and inquiry into the movement of comic or satiric verse in England before the Commonwealth, is beside our present mark. What was properly known, in English and French, as "burlesque verse" was a form of poetic art, strictly defined, which was cultivated for a few years with extravagant zeal, and then dropped. The effect of this form upon subsequent humorous literature was considerable, but indirect, and I need not analyse that here. I will merely try to give a succinct account of the movements, almost simultaneous, which culminated in *Hudibras* with us and in *Le Virgile Travesti* with the French.

Dryden, wishing at once to pay a compliment to Samuel Butler and to deprecate burlesque, showed his fine critical discrimination by saying :

181

" It is indeed below so great a master to make use of such a little instrument." Dryden recognised that burlesque, as used in *Hudibras*, was not a mere accident of expression, but was " a little instrument " of definite character. It consisted of satire, written in short, rapid verse, daringly modern in its language, and entirely devoted to ridicule of persons and matters hitherto regarded as sacred, or at least stately. It had broken out in France in the middle of the seventeenth century, where it was adopted so suddenly that it is difficult to say who introduced it. The name is attributed to Sarrazin, but there seems to be no instance of it earlier than the *Rome Ridicule* of Saint-Amant, which was written in 1643. This piece, a long diatribe against the antiquities of the Eternal City, such as the " *piètre et barbare Colisée, exécrable reste des Goths*," is a violent—and rather amusing—diatribe against the fashionable admiration of the ancient Romans and all their surviving works. It is conceived in the spirit of the modern Futurist, who calls upon his fellow-Italians to fling the leprous palaces of Venice into her stinking canals.

Saint-Amant, who wrote, but did not dare to publish, an equally violent attack on England, where he was for some months French ambassador, shows elsewhere the merits of a real poet. In paradox he was soon outdone by Scarron, who was almost wholly a writer of burlesque, and whose verses are to France what Butler's are to England. Scarron was accompanied by Sarrazin, by a host of

others, even for a moment by Cyrano de Bergerac.
All scribbling France gave itself over to the
manufacture of riotous couplets, strung together
into more or less shapely " poems," all concerned
in ridiculing something or other which had been
universally thought reverend or beautiful.

When this fashion was at its height the Jesuit
critic Vavasseur tried to stem the tide by declaring
that no Greek or Latin writer had ever employed
le genre burlesque, that there was no mention of
it in antiquity, and that Aristotle, Longinus, and
Quintilian had ignored it. He was wrong in his
facts, and he misunderstood the position. It was
because it was recognised as a revolt against the
dignity of ancient tradition that burlesque was so
ardently cultivated. It was welcomed as an act
of defiance, a glove flung by the moderns in the
solemn face of antiquity. Tired of the domina-
tion of the classics, the Parisian public screamed
with delight at seeing Apollo tossed out of his
temple and made to rinse pots in the kitchen.

It really marked the beginning of the great
Quarrel between the Ancients and the Moderns,
which has gone on ever since. The scholastic
tyranny of Greek and Latin had reached a point
where it could be borne no longer, and Scarron
openly declared that classical literature filled him
with horror. He started his series of travesties of
the sacred books of antiquity, and he was rewarded
by a burst of spontaneous merriment. Everybody
knew the text of Virgil, which had been considered
only a little less inspired than the Holy Scriptures.

Scarron therefore started a ridiculous " travesty "
of the *Æneid*. The First Book was received with
sympathetic laughter, and for the next ten years
pedantry, uttering shrieks of pain, was stretched
on the rack of octosyllabic verse. Coarse imitations of the classics, of heroic legend, even of the
Bible, were the rage throughout Paris.

Scarron, who was a genius on a small scale,
had invented something new. The fashion for
burlesque became identified in France with the
Fronde, as it was in England with the Civil War.
In Paris the fury of it lasted ten years ; when
Mazarin returned in 1653 the vogue of burlesque
sank to nothing. Scarron himself turned to other
fields when once the Fronde was over, and the
classic spirit, chastened and modernised, came back
into favour. But the body of Scarron's odes and
travesties and *mazarinades* remained in their
astounding volume and vivacity, and were eagerly
studied abroad when they had already lost their
freshness for Parisian readers. They possessed
one quality distinctly attractive to the English
mind, namely, their realism. It was part of the
system of burlesque to introduce into verse the
names of homely objects, to use words hitherto
considered beneath the dignity of verse, and to
confide to the reader personal details of a kind
hitherto never mentioned.

Scarron, bored by the grammarians, irritated
by the priests, enraged by the political anarchy
of the times, studded his buffooneries with images,
allusions, phrases from low life, which gave spice

to his improvisations and completed the scandal. He had an amazing gift for poetical autobiography; his works, in that age of solemn self-restraint, teem with details about his private doings and the secret life of Paris. The effect was defined by Dryden when he said that burlesque " tickles awkwardly with a kind of pain," but this sort of tickling was already more familiar to the English than to the French habit of mind.

This Scarron fashion of burlesque was discovered in full blast by English Royalists who escaped to Paris during the Fronde. We find that it was accepted by two eminent English writers— by Charles Cotton and by Samuel Butler—to whom we owe its introduction here. But while conditions in France greatly encouraged the immediate production of burlesque, the rule of the Puritans made a delay in its publicity needful in England. Hence—and also because literary life, so minutely recorded in Paris, found hardly an echo in London —we cannot tell exactly when burlesque was brought to us. I have conjectured that Cotton was in Paris about 1648. By that time Scarron had published, tentatively, the First Book of his *Virgile Travesti*. He was not at all sure that it would be well received, but it was, and in course of time he continued his buffoon narrative, prefixing a remarkable epistle to the Chancellor, Seguier.

Cotton appears to have known at first only the earlier publication, and I take this as some faint evidence that his familiarity with it dated from about 1648. I do not know whether it has been observed that Cotton was better acquainted with the contemporary French literature of his youth than any other of the English Royalists. Besides his numerous translations from the *Astrée* of Honoré d'Urfé, which was still extremely popular, he made selected versions of Théophile, Maynard, Racan, and Benserade. The two last he may well have met in person, and it will be noticed that these and others from whom Cotton quotes are the poets whose vogue was at its height before 1650.

The best example of original burlesque which we have in English is, however, the *Hudibras* of Butler, which may have been begun about 1650, but the main structure of which seems to belong to a period after the death of Oliver Cromwell in 1658. What Butler was doing in the long duration of the Rump Parliament is matter of guesswork. If he went to France, as we are told that he did, it must have been before he entered the household of the Puritan scoutmaster, Sir Samuel Luke, under whose shadow Butler hatched in secret his great sectarian satire. Supposing him to be in Paris about 1650, he would find the vogue of burlesque at its height, and Scarron the unquestioned master of it. I confess I cannot agree with those who have ingeniously traced the form of *Hudibras* to Cervantes, to Cleveland, and to the *Satire Ménippée*. There is something of the material and colour of all three in *Hudibras*, but the form seems to be entirely Scarron. The

essence of burlesque, as we have seen, is the
ridicule of matters hitherto held as sacred in short,
rhymed verse, which owes its effect to its rapidity
and reverberation, and to its daring use of realistic
or even vulgar terms in describing matters of
solemnity and dignity. The aim of burlesque
was to set poetry topsy-turvy, and this was done
to perfection by Scarron,

> Qui d'un style rempli de beautés et de charmes,
> Et par d'incomparables vers,
> Fera rire tout l'univers,

as La Mothe le Vayer put it.

We have only to stand the work of Butler and of
Scarron side by side to see how closely the English
poet had studied the manner of the French one.
It is impossible not to wonder whether Butler was
ever admitted to the brilliant salon of the Hotel
de Troyes while all that was witty and desperate
in Paris gathered round the little cripple, who,
huddled in his famous armchair of grey velvet,
defied by his fabulous hilarity the ravages of the
worst arthritic rheumatism on record. Such a
fancy is useless; the living Scarron and Butler could
not have communicated, but the influence of *La
Mazarinade*, I feel sure, quickened into speech the
long-silent genius of the author of *Hudibras*. The
essence of Butler's burlesques is the diffuse and
ample ridicule of things hitherto held sacred. His
most famous book treats the whole Puritan scheme
of religion, politics, and morals as a matter at which
a cat would laugh.

But we may borrow an example less hackneyed than *Hudibras*. The satire on the Royal Society, called *The Elephant in the Moon*, is perhaps the most typical example of burlesque in English. It takes a subject hitherto treated with deserved respect, namely, the spread of scientific research, and pours ridicule upon it in short, vivid couplets with frequent double rhymes. The astronomers gaze through their telescope at the moon, and see an elephant advance into the centre of the luminous orb. This marvellous discovery leads them to a thousand pedantic speculations, until somebody discovers that it is merely a mouse which is creeping over the lens of the instrument. But the learned men are not convinced :

> Some swore, upon a second view,
> That all they'd seen before was true,
> And that they never would recant
> One syllable of th' elephant ;
> Avowed his snout could be no mouse's,
> But a true elephant's proboscis ;
> Others began to doubt and waver,
> Uncertain which o' the two to favour,
> And knew not whether to espouse
> The cause of elephant or mouse.

Apart from direct imitations of *Hudibras*, the vogue of burlesque in England was brief ; it scarcely survived the death of Charles II., to whom was attributed an extreme fondness for this kind of metrical wit. A Puritan divine, the Rev. Robert Wilde, of Aynhoe, cultivated it in strange productions, of which his *Iter Boreale* was the most famous. Wilde approaches very near to the French abandonment, the eager patter of self-betraying rhymes which is so remarkable in Scarron and in Sarrazin :

> Cambridge, now I must leave thee ;
>   And follow Fate !
> College hopes do deceive me ;
>   I oft expected
>   To have been elected,
> But desert is reprobate ;
>   Masters of colleges
>   Have no common graces,
> And they that have fellowships
>   Have but common places,
> And those that scholars are
>   Must have handsome faces ;
> Alas ! poor scholar ! whither wilt thou go ?

The practice of travestying the classics was carried on by Captain Alexander Radcliffe, whose burlesque imitations of Ovid enjoyed a remarkable success. His aim was, frankly, " to blaspheme the best poets " of the classical age, and he bravely declared that, " in his own simple, naked shape," he came nearer to the original than the best of the serious versions. Radcliffe's theory was that " nineteen judicious translators " had not been able to give " the least hint or light into Publius Ovidius Naso's meaning " because of their pomposity and want of humour, and that he was able to do so triumphantly by making the poems homely, colloquial, and modern. Radcliffe, also, we may note in passing, made them very vulgar and indecent, as Cotton made the dialogues of Lucian.

Hudibras escaped this snare, which lay close to the feet of all the other clever and revolutionary versifiers who attempted to destroy the classic tradition, and who for a very brief period succeeded.

"ORION" HORNE

1802–1884

" ORION " HORNE

THE publication of the love letters which passed, in 1845 and 1846, between Robert Browning and Elizabeth Barrett blew a little of the dust off several names which were brightly before the public then and have become sadly obscured since. The two learned lovers speak of Mr. Serjeant Talfourd and of his incomparable tragedy of " Ion," of Sir John Hanmer and his sonnets, of the terrible criticisms of Chorley, of the writings of Abraham Heraud and Silk Buckingham and Cornelius Mathews. These are faded notorieties with a vengeance. But amongst these names, faintly echoing from the earliest Victorian period, we meet with one more than the rest deserving of perpetuation, with at all events a greater mass of actually accomplished work attached to it, the name of Mr. Horne, the author of " Cosmo de Medici," of " Gregory VII.," and, above all, of " the farthing epic," the once extremely celebrated " Orion." And with this there comes vividly back to me a vision of an extraordinary personage, of whom I saw a great deal in my youth, and of whom I feel disposed to garner some of my impressions before I lose them.

He had been baptized Richard Henry Horne, but in late middle life he had changed the second of these names to Hengist. It was in 1874 that

I set eyes on him first, in circumstances which were somewhat remarkable. The occasion was the marriage of the poet, Arthur O'Shaughnessy, to the eldest daughter of Westland Marston, the playwright. There was a large and distinguished company present, and most of the prominent " Pre-Raphaelites," as they were still occasionally called. In the midst of the subsequent festivities, and when the bride was surrounded by her friends, a tiny old gentleman cleared a space around him, and, all uninvited, began to sit upon the floor and sing, in a funny little cracked voice, Spanish songs to his own accompaniment on the guitar. He was very unusual in appearance. Although he was quite bald at the top of his head, his milk-white hair was luxuriant at the sides, and hung in clusters of ringlets. His moustache was so long that it became whisker, and in that condition drooped, also in creamy ringlets, below his chin. The elder guests were inclined to be impatient, the younger to ridicule this rather tactless interruption. Just as it seemed possible something awkward would happen, Robert Browning stepped up and said, in his loud, cheerful voice : " That was charming, Horne ! It quite took us to ' the warm South ' again," and cleverly leading the old gentleman's thoughts to a different topic, he put an end to the incident.

This scene was very characteristic of Horne, who was gay, tactless, and vain to a remarkable degree. He had lately come back from Australia, where nothing had gone well with him for long together, and he did not understand the ways of the younger

generation in London. But to those who could be
patient with his peculiarities he offered a very
amusing study. He had delightful stories, many
of which are still inedited, of the great men of his
youth—Wordsworth, Hunt, Hazlitt, in particular.
But he himself, with his incredible mixture of
affectation and fierceness, humour and absurdity,
enthusiasm and ignorance, with his incoherency of
appearance, at once so effeminate and so muscular,
was better than all his tales. He was a com-
bination of the troubadour and the prize-fighter, on
a miniature scale. It was impossible not to think
of a curly white poodle when one looked at him,
especially when he would throw his fat little person
on a sofa and roll about, with gestures less dignified
than were, perhaps, ever before seen in a poet of
between seventy and eighty years of age. And
yet he had a fine, buoyant spirit, and a generous
imagination with it all. But the oddity of it, alas !
is what lingers in the memory—those milky ringlets,
that extraordinary turn of the head, that embrace
of the beribboned guitar !

In a pathetic little letter which Horne wrote to
me in his eightieth year, he said, quite placidly,
that though he was now forgotten, no poet had
ever had more pleasant things said of him by
people dead and gone. It was perfectly true.
Wordsworth and Tennyson, Leigh Hunt and
Walter Savage Landor, had all praised his poetry ;
Carlyle had declared that " the fire of the stars was
in him," and G. H. Lewes that he was " a man
of the most unquestionable genius." How highly

Robert and Elizabeth Browning regarded him
may be seen over and over again in the course
of their correspondence. But his talent was of
a very fugitive kind. He was a remarkable poet
for seven or eight years, and a tiresome and unin-
spired scribbler for the rest of his life. His period
of good work began in 1837, when he published
" Cosmo de Medici " and " The Death of Mar-
lowe " ; it closed in 1843, with the publication
of " Orion," and the composition of all that was
best in the " Ballad Romances." If anyone
wished to do honour to the *manes* of poor old
Horne—and in these days far less distinguished
poets than he receive the honours of rediscovery—
the way to do it would be to publish in one volume
the very best of his writings, and nothing more.
The badness of the bulk of his later verse is outside
all calculation. How a man who had once written
so well as he, could ever come to write, for instance,
" Bible Tragedies " (1881) is beyond all skill of the
literary historian to comprehend.

But, although Horne was, for a short time, a
good poet, he was always more interesting as a
human being. His whole life was an adventure ;
it was like a " book for boys." He was pleased
to relate that even his birth was not ordinary, for
he came into the world so exactly at the stroke of
midnight on the last day of the year that it could
never be decided whether he was born in 1802 or
1803. I do not know who his parents were or
what his family. In the days when I saw so much
of him he appeared to be quite solitary ; he never

spoke of possessing a relative.   He was trained for
the army, and lost his chance through some foolish
escapade.   But before this he had been at school
at Enfield, where Tom Keats, the poet's brother,
and Charles Wells, who wrote " Joseph and his
Brethren," had been his school-fellows.   He used
to tell us in his old age that he was once scamper-
ing out of school, when he saw the chaise of Mr.
Hammond, the surgeon, standing at the door.
John Keats, who was Hammond's apprentice, was
holding the horse, his head sunken forward in a
brown study ; the boys, who knew how pugnacious
Keats was, dared Horne to throw a snowball at
him, which Horne did, hitting Keats in the back of
the head, and then escaping round the corner at a
headlong pace.   It used to be very thrilling, in the
'eighties, to hear the old gentleman tell how he had
actually snowballed Keats ; almost as though one
should arise and say that he had sold Shakespeare
a cheese-cake.

Just before he should have entered Sandhurst
the young Horne was lured away to America,
and offered himself as a volunteer in the War
of Mexican Independence.   He entered the new
Mexican navy as a midshipman, and dashed about
under irregular fire at the bombardment of Vera
Cruz and at the siege of San Juan Ulloa.   He used
to tell us that he never would miss his swim in the
sea in the morning, nor return to the ship until he
had been well within range of the guns of Vera
Cruz.   The Spaniards could never hit him, he
said ; but one day when he was making a long

nose at the gunners, he was as nearly as possible swallowed from behind by a shark. I forget how he accounted for his escape, but there was always a good deal of Baron Munchausen about Mr. Horne.

When the Mexican War was over, he strolled across the United States, with a belt full of doubloons girded about his person, and visited the Mohawks, the Oneidas, and the Hurons. He had a fight with a Red Indian brave and beat him, and carried away a bunch of eagle-feathers from his body. After many strange adventures, he must needs bathe in public under the cataract of Niagara. Two of his ribs were found to be broken when he was fished out again, insensible. He then took a steerage passage in a steamer that was wrecked in the St. Lawrence. He walked in moccasins over to Halifax, Nova Scotia, and started again in a timber ship, whose crew rose in mutiny and set fire to her in mid-Atlantic ; Mr. Horne quelled the mutiny and put out the fire, to the eternal gratitude of the captain, who fell upon his knees upon the deck and kissed his hands. I delighted in Mr. Horne's stories of his past life, but sometimes I used to fear that he exaggerated.

It was not until he was thirty years of age that Horne began to take up literature, and he was thirty-five when he enjoyed his first success with " Cosmo de Medici," an historical tragedy in blank verse, which has some very fine passages, and was greatly admired in the London coteries. Then came the period of seven years, of which

I have spoken, in which Horne really took his place, with Browning and Tennyson, as one of the promising poets of the age. If he had died in 1844, he would probably hold a high place still, as an "inheritor of unfulfilled renown," but unfortunately he lived for forty more years, and never discovered that his talent had abandoned him. His "Orion," which was published in 1843, was brought out at the price of one farthing. Elizabeth Barrett sent out to the nearest bookshop for a shilling's worth, but was refused her four dozen copies. Purchasers had to produce their brass farthing for each "Orion," and no change was given. This was done "to mark the public contempt into which epic poetry has fallen," but it was also a very good advertisement. Everybody talked about Mr. Horne's "farthing" poem, and after some editions had run out the price was cautiously raised. But when the tenth edition appeared, at a cost of seven shillings, the public perceived that its leg was being pulled, and it purchased "Orion" no more. In spite of all this, "Orion" is far indeed from being a humorous composition ; it is a dignified and melodious romance of Greek symbolism, with some remote relation to the "Hyperion" of Keats, and contains some admirable passages.

The poets of the opening years of Queen Victoria's reign were almost all of them tempted to write philosophical poetry. Robert Browning had led the way with "Pauline" and "Paracelsus." Bailey had produced "Festus"; Ragg, the lace-worker (now forgotten), had made a temporary mark with " The Deity," a formidable essay ; Miss Barrett wrote " The Drama of Exile " ; there were the lucubrations of John Edmund Reade. None of these laborious poems could be styled successful, but they all were interesting in their curious contemporary effort to reconcile ideas with sensations, on a grand scale. These writers believed that unless a poem contained a philosophy it was, on the whole, a poor affair. Horne joined the band of the philosophers when he wrote " Orion," which is perhaps, as a poem, the best of the group. His mind was not disciplined, but he always had a curiosity about the literature of thought. He made the acquaintance, about 1841, of a doctor of philosophy, Dr. Leonard Schmitz, who came over from Bonn to introduce German literature to English readers. Conversation with Schmitz set Horne's thoughts running in the direction of a poem which should re-establish the union which had existed in ancient times between philosophy and poetry, before analysis stepped in and divorced them. The effort was one quite beyond Horne's power to carry out successfully, but he wrote what is by no means the worst of modern machines.

This is the poet's explanation of his " spiritual epic," as Elizabeth Barrett called it, as it appeared to him thirty years afterwards :

" Orion, the hero of my fable, is meant to present a type of the struggle of man with himself —that is to say, the contest between the intellect and the senses, when powerful energies are equally balanced. Orion is man standing naked before Heaven and Destiny, resolved to work as a really free agent to the utmost pitch of his powers for the good of his race. He is a truly practical believer in his gods and in his own conscience ; a man with the strength of a giant ; innocently wise ; with a heart expanding towards the largeness and warmth of Nature, and a spirit unconsciously aspiring to the stars. He is a dreamer of noble dreams and a hunter of grand shadows (in accordance with the ancient symbolic myth), all tending to healthy thought or to practical action and structure. He is the type of a Worker and a Builder for his fellow-men."

There is in this commentary a touch of the teaching of Carlyle, who in his turn perused " Orion " with marked affability. The sage of Chelsea had recently published *Heroes and Hero-worship*, which had no warmer admirer than Horne. " Orion," then, the " farthing epic," appeared with every circumstance in its favour and enjoyed a very considerable success. Why it is no longer read it would be difficult to say. Its lustrous descriptions of primeval giants are solemn and beautiful, but unfortunately the memory goes back to " Hyperion." Yet this is unjust, and it would be puzzling to define what it is that makes so very careful and accomplished a work not any longer easy to read, in spite of its excellent proportions, moderate length, and indisputable dignity. The " deliberate opinion " of

Edgar Allan Poe was that " in all that regards the loftiest and holiest attributes of true poetry ' Orion ' has never been excelled." It is certainly very good ; listen :

> Ye rocky heights of Chios, where the snow,
> Lit by the far-off and receding moon,
> Now feels the soft dawn's purpling twilight creep
> Over your ridges, while the mystic dews
> Swarm down and wait to be instinct with gold
> And solar fire !—ye mountains waving brown
> With thick-winged woods, and blotted with deep caves
> In secret places ; and ye paths that stray
> E'en as ye list ; what odours and what sighs
> Tend your sweet silence through the star-showered night,
> Like memories breathing of the Goddess-forms
> That left your haunts, yet with the day return.

Excellent, until we come to the last two lines, which are invaded by that curious flatness characteristic of English poetry in the unfortunate reign of King William IV. When Douglas Jerrold said that Horne had " presented an undying gift to the world " in " Orion," he forgot to estimate the element of decomposition involved in the language of all metrical writers between Keats and Tennyson. Darley, Wade, Wells, Bailey, Heraud, and Beddoes—they all had the unfortunate crack in the voice which made them, with their wealth of enthusiasm for the grand style, incapable of carrying it out without incessant lapses into mediocrity of expression. And Horne, to use a vulgar expression, is tarred with the same William IV. brush. Yet there are very good things in " Orion," lines such as :

'Tis always morning somewhere in the world,

and passages of Greek landscape, of which this is
by no means an isolated example :

> since the breath of spring had stirred the woods,
> Through which the joyous tidings busily ran,
> And oval buds of delicate pink and green
> Broke, infant-like, through bark of sapling boughs,—
> The vapours from the ocean had ascended,
> Fume after fume, wreath after wreath, and floor
> On floor, till a grey curtain upward spread
> From sea to sky, and both as one appeared.
> Now came the snorting and intolerant steeds
> Of the Sun's chariot towards the summer signs ;
> At first obscurely, then with dazzling beams,

and so on. And, as some one has said of La-
martine's efforts in the same kind, there is throughout " Orion," if not a philosophy, at all events a
creditable movement of philosophical reflection.

It is known to Apollo only what varied employ-
ments Horne took up when the Muses began to
abandon him. He was sub-editor of *Household
Words* under Dickens, and special commissioner
of the *Daily News* to Ireland when the great
famine broke out. Suddenly, and desperately
determined to marry, he went down to stay with
Miss Mitford in Berkshire, and proposed to all
the neighbouring heiresses one after another, to
the intense indignation of that lady, who declared
that he had used her hospitable dining-room, on
the same day, to propose to a lady (with £50,000
a year) at lunch, and to another (with £40,000 a
year) at tea. None of these efforts was crowned

with success ; perhaps he had the presumption to be in love with Elizabeth Barrett, whom he had at that time never seen, although oceans of correspondence had passed between them. At all events, directly Robert Browning had carried off his eminent bride, Horne appeared with a little Miss Foggs upon his arm, whom he presently married. They did not get on together ; why should history conceal the fact, when Horne himself was wont to dilate upon it so freely to his friends ? Mrs. Horne, in tears, threw herself upon the paternal sympathy of Charles Dickens, and Horne indignantly sought a southern hemisphere.

In Australia he was commander of the Gold Escort, and it was delightful, years afterwards, to hear him tell how he convoyed several tons of bullion from Ballarat to Melbourne amid every circumstance of peril. Then he became Gold Commissioner to the Government, but here his flow of high spirits carried him away. He then flung himself into the cultivation of the cochineal insect, edited a Victorian newspaper, became Commissioner of Waterworks, gave lessons in gymnastics, professed the art of natation, and was one of the starters of Australian wine-growing. Long afterwards, when the first Australian cricketers came over to England, Horne wrote to me : " I learn that the cricketers have made *each* £1000 over here ! Why, oh ! why did not I become an Australian cricketer, instead of an unprofitable swimmer ? When years no longer smiled upon my balls and runs, I might have retired upon my laurelled bat, and have published tragedies at my own expense. Is there any redress for these things in another world ? I don't think so ; I shall be told I had my choice." He certainly paid his money. No one, I suppose, ever failed in so many brilliant, unusual enterprises, every one of which was sure to succeed when he adopted it.

When he came back from Australia, I think about 1869, he was in low water. He had managed very deeply to offend Charles Dickens, who had taken up the cause of Horne's neglected wife. What happened to Horne in the early years after his return I never heard ; I fancy that he went abroad again for some part of the time. A little later Robert Browning, who had always felt a sincere regard for Horne, was able to be of practical service to him. He was encouraged to republish his poems, and to appeal by means of them to the new age. In these days one used to meet him at afternoon parties, carrying with great care, under his arm, the precious guitar, which he called " my daughter," and was used ceremoniously to introduce as " Miss Horne." A little later in the evening Horne would be discovered on a low stool, warbling Mexican romances, or murmuring with exaggerated gallantry to the prettiest girl in the room. All this time he was thirsting for publicity—if he could only be engaged to sing in public, to box in public, to swim in public, how happy he would be ! It used to be said that when he was nearly seventy Horne persuaded the captain of a ship to tie his legs together and fling him into the sea, and that he swam with ease to the boat. A wonderful little ringleted athlete, no doubt !

A great deal of Horne's work in verse, and even in prose, remains unpublished, and is not very likely, I thould think, to be ever printed. As I have said, his faculty, which had been so graceful, faded away from him about forty years before he died. When he was in Australia he wrote a good deal, among other things a choral drama, "Prometheus, the Fire-Bringer," which was actually composed out in the bush, and lost, and written all over again, still in the bush. The first edition of this poem is styled " by Richard *Henry* Horne," and the second, which followed soon after, " by Richard *Hengist* Horne," showing the period at which he adopted the more barbaric name. I have glanced through a mass of Horne's manuscript, which I possess (I believe that Mr. Buxton Forman possesses a great deal more), to see whether I can find anything unpublished which is good enough to offer to the readers of this volume. The following impromptu is at least brief ; it was composed when the poet was in his seventy-eighth year :

THE SPRING-TIDE OF THE BARDS

Ah, where is the Spring-tide of Poets of old,
　When Chaucer lov'd April and all her sweet showers,
When Spenser's knights felt not their armour strike cold,
　Tho' lost in wet forests or dreaming in bowers ?

"ORION" HORNE

'Tis a far other planet to us in this season,
And Nature must own we complain with some reason

For north winds, and east winds, and yellow-fac'd fogs,
  And thunders and lightnings that scare buds and shoots,
May cheer the hoarse chorus of cold-blooded frogs,
  But Man craves life's future, and fears for its fruits.
Then come again, Spring, like the dear songs of old,
Where the crocus smiled daily in sunlight and gold.

Horne's cheerfulness was a very pleasant feature in his character. Life had treated him scurvily, love had missed him, fame had come down and crowned him, and then had rudely snatched the laurel away. If ever a man might have been excused for sourness, it was Horne. But he was a gallant little old man, and if it was impossible not to smile at him, it was still less possible not to recognise his courage and his spirit. Curiously enough, Elizabeth Barrett, who carried on so close a correspondence with Horne in her unmarried days, but who, warned by Miss Mitford, never would allow him to call upon her in person, had an accurate instinct of his merits and his weaknesses, and all the casual remarks about Horne which she makes in the course of her letters to Robert Browning strike one who knew Horne well in later years as singularly exact and perspicacious. His edition of her letters to him, published about twenty years ago in two volumes, is becoming a rare book, and contains many things of remarkable interest and importance.

It was from 1876 to 1879 that we saw him most frequently. He was living at this time in two rooms in Northumberland Street, Regent's Park, in very great poverty, which he bore with the gayest and most gallant *insouciance*. An attempt was made—indeed, several attempts were made—to secure for him a little pension from the Civil List, and these were supported by Carlyle and Browning, Tennyson and Swinburne, to name no smaller fry. But all in vain ; for some reason, absolutely inscrutable to me, these efforts were of no avail. It was darkly said that there were reasons why Mr. Gladstone would never, never yield ; and he never did. When Lord Beaconsfield came into office, he granted the poor little old man £50 a year, but even then he had not too much food to eat nor clothes to keep him warm. Still he went bravely on, shaking his white ringlets and consoling himself with his guitar. He was fond of mystery, which is a great consoler. For economy's sake, he used to write on post-cards, but always with a great deal of care, so that the postman should be none the wiser. I have such a post-card before me now ; it is an answer to a proposal of mine that he should come in and take dinner with us :

"*Nov.* 29, 1877.

" The Sharpshooter's friendly shot just received. By adroitly porting my helm, and hauling out my flying jib, I shall, by 7 o'clock this evening, be able to get the weather-gauge of the Cape I was bound for, and run into your Terrace. Thine.

" REEFER."

Nothing, surely, could be more discreet than that.

To the very last he was anxious to regain his old place as a man of letters, and his persistency was really quite pathetic. One did not know what to do with his suggestions. I appeal to anyone acquainted with the business of literature whether anything can be more trying than to receive this sort of communication :

" Don't you think curiosity might be aroused if you could induce the editor of the *Athenæum* to print something of this kind : ' We understand that a leading periodical will shortly contain a Dramatic Scene by the Author of " Orion," entitled " The Circle of the Regicides," in which such interlocutors as Dr. Kobold, Prof. Franz Tollkopf, Hans Arbeitsdulder, and Baron Dumm von Ehrsucht will represent certain well-known characters. There will also be brought upon the scene the Apparitions of Brutus, Cromwell, the patriot Mazzini, and the philanthropist Robert Owen ; together with a chorus of French and Russian revolutionists, with a trio and chorus of female Regicides.' On second thoughts, perhaps better stop after ' Owen.' ' "

It was difficult to bring such suggestions as these within the range of practical literature.

Horne's physical strength was very extraordinary in old age. It was strangely incompatible with the appearance of the little man, with his ringleted locks and mincing ways. But he was past seventy before he ceased to challenge powerful young swimmers to feats of natation, and he very often beat them, carrying off from them cups and medals, to their deep disgust. He was nearly eighty when he filled us, one evening, with alarm by bending our drawing-room poker to an angle in striking it upon the strained muscles of his fore-arm. He was very vain of his physical accomplishments, and he used to declare that he was in training to be a centenarian. These are things that should never be said, they tempt the fates; so one day, just after poor Mr. Horne had been boasting, he was knocked down by a van in Lisson Grove, and, although he rallied in a wonderful way, he was never the same man again. Presently, on March 13, 1884, he died at Margate, whither he had been removed to take the benefit of the sea air. He was in his eighty-second year. It would be a great pity that a man so unique and so picturesque should be forgotten. As long as the world is interested in Elizabeth Barrett Browning, Horne can never be entirely forgotten, but he deserves to be remembered for his own sake.

EDGAR POE AND HIS
DETRACTORS

EDGAR POE AND HIS
DETRACTORS

THERE is a homely proverb which tells us that
some cats would rather be stroked the wrong way
than not stroked at all. If Poe belonged to this
feline category, and it is evident that he did, his
ghost must feel no reason to be dissatisfied with the
history of the last seventy years. Where are the
flattered rivals who caused him so much anxiety?
Who now remembers Epes Sargent, or who is
moved by Pendleton Cooke of Virginia ? They
are as if they had never been, while Poe, whose
sleep their laurels troubled, is one of the most
universally discussed of the authors of the nineteenth century. Of American authors he has
certainly been the most discussed, and in the long
run the heated controversy about his vices and his
plagiarisms and his morbidity has been of immense
help to his reputation. If this cat has been stroked
the wrong way, his fur has, at all events, cast off
sparks of electricity which have made a fine blaze
of notoriety all around him ; and it happens that
he was a man of genius as well.

It is a commonplace to say that England perceived the light of Poe while America still lay in
darkness. But it is not so usual to admit that
France was also in the forefront of appreciation.

Baudelaire and Mallarmé made Poe a French
classic in their marvellous translations of his prose
and verse when his fame at home was yet very
unsteady. It is now again a Frenchman who
comes forward with a fine contribution to his biography. M. André Fontainas is a Belgian by birth
(he was born in Brussels in 1865), but he came very
early to Paris, and is now completely French. He
is a poet of rare delicacy and distinction, author
of many volumes, of which the first, *Le Sang des
Fleurs*, showed his discipleship to Mallarmé, whose
close associate he was. It may well be that Mallarmé, by his zeal for Poe, awakened his young
Flemish friend's enthusiasm ; but M. Fontainas,
who has translated the poems of Milton, Keats,
and George Meredith, needs no guide in English
literature. He has now published a life of Edgar
Poe which, although far from the longest, is
probably the best that has yet appeared in any
language. The facts are stated here succinctly,
with reference to the very latest investigations, and
we get as precise and full an account of the actual
life of the poet, several passages of which must
always remain mysterious, as we are ever likely
to secure.

A fervent apology for the much - belaboured
bard is what M. Fontainas sets out to present, and
it is possible to conclude that his indulgence is
occasionally excessive. The balance is held with
difficulty, but it was preserved successfully, on the
whole, by the late John H. Ingram, whose death at
Brighton in 1916 (an event unrecorded at the time)

removed a man who had devoted himself almost exclusively to the elucidation of Poe's life and works during five-and-forty years, and whose name must always be mentioned with honour by lovers of the poet. M. Fontainas, of course, leans much on Ingram, and he acknowledges due help from the profuse labours of a cloud of American investigators during the last ten years, by whom a formidable mass of Transatlantic material, still much in need of the winnowing-fan, has been collected. That there should be so much mystification, and that it should be so difficult, and yet possible, to get fresh information about a man of letters who lived in places like New York, Philadelphia, and Baltimore less than a hundred years ago, is only to be understood when we realise that Poe was a typical product, on his commonplace side, of the *Martin Chuzzlewit* period of American civilisation. He lived in a whirl of mental activity where most of the figures were of infusorial size, in a country whose bubbling passion found a vent in such enlightened channels as *Burton's Gentlemen's Magazine* and *The Whig Review*. If we were to call up Poe as a social character of his age, he would probably arise before us a ring-tailed roarer at the Great Meeting of the Watertoast Sympathisers. He lived among the Zephaniah Scadders and the La Fayette Kettles of that appalling time, and his memory has to be retrieved, piecemeal, out of the dust-heap of their remains.

But Poe was himself responsible for a great deal

of the mystification. Autobiographical truth was
not in him, and the lies he told about himself have
kept busy a hundred pens. When he thought he
was dying, in 1847, he dictated from his bed a
simple record of his own life's story, which was a
hoax in almost every particular. He described
his travels in Greece and his adventures on board
a whaler ; he told how he fought a duel in Paris
and starved in London. Commentators have worn
themselves out in trying to follow up these indications. Vain efforts, for Poe never went to Greece,
and never saw a whaler, and never fought a duel.
He was in lodgings in Boston, Mass., all the time.
A French critic, M. Lauvrière, has built up a whole
fabric on the statement that when Mrs. Stannard,
the earliest of Poe's loves, died, the poet spent long,
horrible nights exposed to icy rain and bitter wind
in the abandoned graveyard where she lay. It
now appears that he was fourteen years of age at
the time, and well looked after in an eminently
respectable boarding-school.

Poe's love for practical jokes has been his own
undoing, and the source of his posthumous misfortunes. His grimmest and insanest hoax was
making the Rev. Rufus Griswold his literary
executor. Griswold is an insect that would be
completely forgotten were it not eternally em-
balmed in the amber of Poe's romance. He was
a tenth-rate critic, versifier, editor, and man-of-
all-work whom Poe met when he went to settle
at Philadelphia in 1841. The relations between
the two men have lately been worked out with

scrupulous minuteness by Professor Killis Campbell in his valuable pamphlet on " The Poe - Griswold Controversy." For the first year nothing but compliments passed when these gentlemen met. Then there was a violent change, and Poe described a work of Griswold's as " a very muttonish production " and its author as " one of the most clumsy of literary thieves." In 1845 they were in each other's arms again ; in 1846 Poe discovered that Griswold had been " backbiting " him ; all again was rage and fury, and Griswold openly attacked " The Raven." There was now no man whom Poe despised and hated more, although in 1849 he seems to have asked him for pecuniary help. But when he died, on October 7 of that year, he was found to have requested the very Griswold, about whom he had been " witheringly severe," to serve as his literary executor. It was the last and worst of all his series . of practical jokes.

Griswold leaped upon the corpse like a ghoul. His chance had come to magnify himself and wipe out the insolence of Poe's satire. On the second day after the poet's death there appeared in the *New York Tribune*, over the signature " Ludwig," an article which has at last been traced to Griswold, in which the character of Poe was mercilessly exposed. The precious executor, however, was not courting obscurity, for in the following January he published his edition of Poe's Works, in two volumes, prefixed by a signed Memoir in which he gave a fancy sketch of the poet as a sort of devil, stained by every vice, incapable of friendship, arrogant, choleric, devoid of honour, and so spiteful that " his cheek paled with gnawing envy if you spoke to him of wealth." That Poe had contrived to make himself thoroughly disliked by a large circle of journalists is obvious fron the fact, which Mr. Killis Campbell expands, that at first very few friends came forward to rebut the charges which Griswold had made, while there were plenty of people ready to protest that it was very sad, and that they had known it all along. It is true that the poet's sister, Rosalie Poe, described Griswold's Memoir as the most " atrocious instance of human iniquity since the days of Cain." But she was held to be biassed, and Griswold, the honest executor, to whom truth was above all worldly considerations, long held his ground.

Let us examine the charges that have been brought against Poe during these last seventy years. I cannot agree with M. Fontainas in holding that Poe was a spotless lamb. Yet I am even more at variance with the Griswold gang, who see in him a coal-black sheep. That he had a weak head, and often drank too much, is, I am afraid, certain ; but, after all, Mr. Pussyfoot had not then been appointed the American Lord Chief Justice. That Poe was a sad philanderer is another charge which must be admitted proven. He made love to many women, but he did none of them any harm. They all liked it very much. There were at least a dozen of them, and the pride of each in after-memories of his attention was only equalled by her hatred of the other eleven. What Poe sought for was a mother rather than a mistress ; " only a bosom to rest on," as another poet has put it ; and his chief fault was hurrying so incontinently from pillow to pillow. Then we are told that he had no sense of honour, that he was always borrowing money, and that he was rude when he was asked to return it. Doubtless the poor man would have been only too glad to pay his debts, but he could not. I am sorry that he borrowed from people whom he had just attacked, and whom he proceeded to praise, and then, when he had spent the money, to attack again. I am afraid he did not always behave like a little gentleman, but it is not given to every one to be as Mr. Micawber was, incurably insolvent, yet permanently gentlemanlike. Griswold wrote that Poe's life was passed " without a recognition or a manifestation of conscience." But from what sort of glass-house did Griswold throw stones ?

The story of Poe's life will always be interesting, because there are elements in it which are incongruous, and others which are still a mystery. (It is very remarkable that the investigation of a hundred searchers should leave us still quite in the dark as to how and where Poe spent the last five days of his life !) When he himself said that it is " paradoxical to speak of a man of genius as personally ignoble," he was probably thinking of the wretched circumstances in which his life was cast, and the squalor which they reflected on his weakness. But when we contemplate the mean and flatulent society which surrounded him, and then his own exquisite genius, we are ready to forgive not only his actual faults, but even the crimes which the egregious Griswold invented for his dishonour.

THOMAS HARDY'S LYRICAL
POETRY

THE LYRICAL POETRY OF THOMAS HARDY

WHEN, about Christmas time in 1898, Mr. Hardy's admirers, who were expecting from him a new novel, received instead a thick volume of verse, there was mingled with their sympathy and respect a little disappointment and a great failure in apprehension. Those who were not rude enough to suggest that a cobbler should stick to his last, reminded one another that many novelists had sought relaxation by trifling with the Muses. Thackeray had published *Ballads*, and George Eliot had expatiated in a *Legend of Jubal*. No one thought the worse of *Coningsby* because its author had produced a *Revolutionary Epic*. It took some time for even intelligent criticism to see that the new *Wessex Poems* did not fall into this accidental category, and still, after twenty years, there survives a tendency to take the verse of Mr. Hardy, abundant and solid as it has become, as a mere subsidiary and ornamental appendage to his novels. It is still necessary to insist on the complete independence of his career as a poet, and to point out that if he had never published a page of prose he would deserve to rank high among the writers of his country on the score of the eight volumes of his verse. It is as a lyrical poet, and

223

solely as a lyrical poet, that I propose to speak of him to-day.

It has been thought extraordinary that Cowper was over fifty when he published his first secular verses, but Mr. Hardy was approaching his sixtieth year when he sent *Wessex Poems* to the press. Such self-restraint—" none hath by more studious ways endeavoured, and with more unwearied spirit none shall "—has always fascinated the genuine artist, but few have practised it with so much tenacity. When the work of Mr. Hardy is completed, nothing, it is probable, will more strike posterity than its unity, its consistency. He has given proof, as scarce any other modern writer has done, of tireless constancy of resolve. His novels formed an unbroken series from the *Desperate Remedies* of 1871 to *The Well-Beloved* of 1897. In the fullness of his success, and unseduced by all temptation, he closed that chapter of his career, and has kept it closed. Since 1898 he has been, persistently and periodically, a poet and nothing else. That he determined, for reasons best left to his own judgement, to defer the exhibition of his verse until he had completed his work in prose, ought not to prejudice criticism in its analysis of the lyrics and the colossal dramatic panorama. Mr. Hardy, exclusively as a poet, demands our undivided attention.

It is legitimate to speculate on other probable causes of Mr. Hardy's delay. From such information as lies scattered before us, we gather that it was from 1865 to 1867 that he originally took poetry to be his vocation. The dated pieces in the volume of 1898 help us to form an idea of the original character of his utterance. On the whole it was very much what it remains in the pieces composed after a lapse of half a century. Already, as a very young man, Mr. Hardy possessed his extraordinary insight into the movements of human character, and his eloquence in translating what he had observed of the tragedy and pain of rustic lives. No one, for sixty years, had taken so closely to heart the admonitions of Wordsworth in his famous Preface to the 1800 edition of *Lyrical Ballads* to seek for inspiration in that condition where " the passions of men are incorporated with the beautiful forms of nature." But it may well be doubted whether Mr. Hardy's poems would have been received in the mid-Victorian age with favour, or even have been comprehended. Fifty years ahead of his time, he was asking in 1866 for novelty of ideas, and he must have been conscious that his questioning would seem inopportune. He needed a different atmosphere, and he left the task of revolt to another, and, at first sight, a very unrelated force, that of the *Poems and Ballads* of the same year. But Swinburne succeeded in his revolution, and although he approached the art from an opposite direction, he prepared the way for an ultimate appreciation of Mr. Hardy.

We should therefore regard the latter, in spite of his silence of forty years, as a poet who laboured, like Swinburne, at a revolution against the optimism and superficial sweetness of his age. Swinburne, it is true, tended to accentuate the poetic side of poetry, while Mr. Hardy drew verse, in some verbal respects, nearer to prose. This does not affect their common attitude, and the sympathy of these great artists for one another's work has already been revealed, and will be still more clearly exposed. But they were unknown to each other in 1866, when to both of them the cheap philosophy of the moment, the glittering femininity of the " jewelled line," the intense respect for Mrs. Grundy in her Sunday satin, appeared trumpery, hateful, and to be trampled upon. We find in Mr. Hardy's earliest verse no echo of the passionate belief in personal immortality which was professed by Ruskin and Browning. He opposed the Victorian theory of human " progress " ; the Tennysonian beatific Vision seemed to him ridiculous. He rejected the idea of the sympathy and goodness of Nature, and was in revolt against the self-centredness of the Romantics. We may conjecture that he combined a great reverence for *The Book of Job* with a considerable contempt for *In Memoriam*.

This was not a mere rebellious fancy which passed off ; it was something inherent that remained, and gives to-day their peculiar character to Mr. Hardy's latest lyrics. But before we examine the features of this personal mode of interpreting poetry to the world, we may collect what little light we can on the historic develop-

ment of it.   In the pieces dated between 1865 and
1867 we find the germ of almost everything which
has since characterised the poet.   In " Amabel "
the ruinous passage of years, which has continued
to be an obsession with Mr. Hardy, is already
crudely dealt with.   The habit of taking poetical
negatives of small scenes—" your face, and the
God-curst sun, and a tree, and a pond edged with
grayish leaves " (" Neutral Times ")—which had
not existed in English verse since the days of
Crabbe, reappears.   There is marked already a
sense of terror and resentment against the blind
motions of chance—in " Hap " the author would
positively welcome a certainty of divine hatred
as a relief from the strain of depending upon
" crass casualty."   Here and there in these earliest
pieces an extreme difficulty of utterance is remarkable in the face of the ease which the poet attained
afterwards in the expression of his most strange
images and fantastic revelations.   We read in
" At a Bridal " :

> Should I, too, wed as slave to Mode's decree,
> And each thus found apart, of false desire
> A stolid line, whom no high aims will fire
> As had fired ours could ever have mingled we !

This, although perfectly reducible, takes time to
think out, and at a hasty glance seems muffled
up in obscurity beyond the darkness of Donne ;
moreover, it is scarcely worthy in form of the
virtuoso which Mr. Hardy was presently to become.
Perhaps of the poems certainly attributable to

this earliest period, the little cycle of sonnets called " She to Him " gives clearest promise of what was coming. The sentiment is that of Ronsard's famous " Quand vous serez bien vieille, au soir, à la chandelle," but turned round, as Mr. Hardy loves to do, from the man to the woman, and embroidered with ingenuities, such as where the latter says that as her temperament dies down the habit of loving will remain, and she be

> Numb as a vane that cankers on its point,
> True to the wind that kissed ere canker came,

which attest a complexity of mind that Ronsard's society knew nothing of.

On the whole, we may perhaps be safe in conjecturing that whatever the cause, the definite dedication to verse was now postponed. Meanwhile, the writing of novels had become the business of Mr. Hardy's life, and ten years go by before we trace a poet in that life again. But it is interesting to find that when the great success of *Far from the Madding Crowd* had introduced him to a circle of the best readers, there followed an effect which again disturbed his ambition for the moment. Mr. Hardy was once more tempted to change the form of his work. He wished " to get back to verse," but was dissuaded by Leslie Stephen, who induced him to start writing *The Return of the Native* instead. On March 29, 1875, Coventry Patmore, then a complete stranger, wrote to express his regret that " such almost unequalled beauty and power as appeared in the novels should not have assured themselves the immortality which would have been conferred upon them by the form of verse." This was just at the moment when we find Mr. Hardy's conversations with " long Leslie Stephen in the velveteen coat " obstinately turning upon " theologies decayed and defunct, the origin of things, the constitution of matter, and the unreality of time." To this period belongs also the earliest conception of *The Dynasts*, an old note-book containing, under the date June 20, 1875, the suggestion that the author should attempt "An Iliad of Europe from 1789 to 1815."

To this time also seems to belong the execution of what has proved the most attractive section of Mr. Hardy's poetry, the narratives, or short Wessex ballads. The method in which these came into the world is very curious. Many of these stories were jotted down to the extent of a stanza or two when the subject first occurred to the author. For instance, " The Fire at Tranter Sweatley's," first published by Lionel Johnson in 1894, had been begun as early as 1867, and was finished ten years later. The long ballad of " Leipzig " and the savage " San Sebastian," both highly characteristic, were also conceived and a few lines of each noted down long before their completion. " Valenciennes," however, belongs to 1878, and the " Dance at the Phœnix," of which the stanza beginning " 'Twas Christmas " alone had been written years before, seems to have been

finished about the same time. What evidence is
before us goes to prove that in the 'seventies Mr.
Hardy became a complete master of the art of
verse, and that his poetic style was by this time
fixed. He still kept poetry out of public sight,
but he wrote during the next twenty years, as
though in a backwater off the stream of his novels,
the poems which form the greater part of the volume
of 1898. If no other collection of his lyrical verse
existed, we should miss a multitude of fine things,
but our general conception of his genius would
be little modified.

We should judge carelessly, however, if we
treated the subsequent volumes as mere repetitions
of the original *Wessex Poems*. They present
interesting differences, which I may rapidly note
before I touch on the features which characterise
the whole body of Mr. Hardy's verse. *Poems
of the Past and Present*, which came out in the
first days of 1902, could not but be in a certain
measure disappointing, in so far as it paralleled
its three years' product with that of the thirty
years of *Wessex Poems*. Old pieces were published in it, and it was obvious that in 1898
Mr. Hardy might be expected to have chosen
from what used to be called his " portfolio " those
specimens which he thought to be most attractive. But on further inspection this did not
prove to be quite the case. After pondering for
twelve years on the era of Napoleon, his pre-
occupation began in 1887 to drive him into
song :

THOMAS HARDY

Must I pipe a palinody,
Or be silent thereupon ?

He decides that silence has become impossible :

Nay ; I'll sing " The Bridge of Lodi "—
That long-loved, romantic thing,
Though none show by smile or nod, he
Guesses why and what I sing !

Here is the germ of *The Dynasts*. But in the
meantime the crisis of the Boer War had cut
across the poet's dream of Europe a hundred years
ago, and a group of records of the Dorsetshire
elements of the British army at the close of 1899
showed in Mr. Hardy's poetry what had not been
suspected there—a military talent of a most remarkable kind. Another set of pieces composed
in Rome were not so interesting ; Mr. Hardy
always seems a little languid when he leaves the
confines of his native Wessex. Another section of
Poems of the Past and Present is severely, almost
didactically, metaphysical, and expands in varied
language the daring thought, so constantly present
in Mr. Hardy's reverie, that God Himself has forgotten the existence of earth, this " tiny sphere,"
this " tainted ball," " so poor a thing," and has
left all human life to be the plaything of blind
chance. This sad conviction is hardly ruffled by
" The Darkling Thrush," which goes as far
towards optimism as Mr. Hardy can let himself
be drawn, or by such reflections as those in " On
a Fine Morning " :

Whence comes Solace ? Not from seeing
What is doing, suffering, being ;

Not from noting Life's conditions,
Not from heeding Time's monitions ;
  But in cleaving to the Dream,
  And in gazing on the gleam
  Whereby gray things golden seem.

Eight years more passed, years marked by the stupendous effort of *The Dynasts*, before Mr. Hardy put forth another collection of lyrical poems. *Time's Laughingstocks* confirmed, and more than confirmed, the high promise of *Wessex Poems*. The author, in one of his modest prefaces, where he seems to whisper while we bend forward in our anxiety not to miss one thrifty sentence, expresses the hope that *Time's Laughingstocks* will, as a whole, take the " reader forward, even if not far, rather than backward."

The book, indeed, does not take us " far " forward, simply because the writer's style and scope were definitely exposed to us already, and yet it does take us " forward," because the hand of the master is conspicuously firmer and his touch more daring. The *Laughingstocks* themselves are fifteen in number, tragical stories of division and isolation, of failures in passion, of the treason of physical decay. No landscape of Mr. Hardy's had been more vivid than the night - pictures in " The Revisitation," where the old soldier in barracks creeps out on to the gaunt down, and meets (by one of Mr. Hardy's coincidences) his ancient mistress, and no picture more terrible than the revelation of each to the other in a blaze of sunrise. What a document for the future is " Reminiscences of a Dancing Man " ? If only

Shakespeare could have left us such a song of the London in 1585 ! But the power of the poet culminates in the pathos of " The Tramp Woman " —perhaps the greatest of all Mr. Hardy's lyrical poems—and in the horror of "A Sunday Morning's Tragedy."

It is noticeable that *Time's Laughingstocks* is, in some respects, a more daring collection than its predecessors. We find the poet here entirely emancipated from convention, and guided both in religion and morals exclusively by the inner light of his reflection. His energy now interacts on his clairvoyance with a completeness which he had never quite displayed before, and it is here that we find Mr. Hardy's utterance peculiarly a quintessence of himself. Especially in the narrative pieces—which are often Wessex novels distilled into a wine-glass, such as " Rose-Ann," and " The Vampirine-Fair "—he allows no considerations of what the reader may think " nice " or " pleasant " to shackle his sincerity or his determination ; and it is therefore to *Time's Laughingstocks* that the reader who wishes to become intimately acquainted with Mr. Hardy as a moralist most frequently recurs. We notice here more than elsewhere in his poems Mr. Hardy's sympathy with the local music of Wessex, and especially with its expression by the village choir, which he uses as a spiritual symbol. Quite a large section of *Time's Laughingstocks* takes us to the old-fashioned gallery of some church, where the minstrels are bowing " New Sabbath " or

"Mount Ephraim," or to a later scene where the ghosts in whose melancholy apparition Mr. Hardy takes such pleasure, chant their goblin melodies and strum "the viols of the dead" in the moonlit churchyard. The very essence of Mr. Hardy's reverie at this moment of his career is to be found, for instance, in "The Dead Quire," where the ancient phantom-minstrels revenge themselves on their gross grandsons outside the alehouse.

Almost immediately after the outbreak of the present war Mr. Hardy presented to a somewhat distraught and inattentive public another collection of his poems. It cannot be said that *Satires of Circumstance* is the most satisfactory of those volumes ; it is, perhaps, that which we could with the least discomposure persuade ourselves to overlook. Such a statement refers more to the high quality of other pages than to any positive decay of power or finish here. There is no less adroitness of touch and penetration of view in this book than elsewhere, and the poet awakens once more our admiration by his skill in giving poetic value to minute conditions of life which have escaped less careful observers. But in *Satires of Circumstance* the ugliness of experience is more accentuated than it is elsewhere, and is flung in our face with less compunction. The pieces which give name to the volume are only fifteen in number, but the spirit which inspires them is very frequently repeated in other parts of the collection. That spirit is one of mocking sarcasm, and it acts in every case by presenting a beautifully draped figure of illusion, from which the poet, like a sardonic showman, twitches away the robe that he may display a skeleton beneath it.

We can with little danger assume, as we read the *Satires of Circumstance*, hard and cruel shafts of searchlight as they seem, that Mr. Hardy was passing through a mental crisis when he wrote them. This seems to be the *Troilus and Cressida* of his life's work, the book in which he is revealed most distracted by conjecture and most over-whelmed by the miscarriage of everything. The wells of human hope have been poisoned for him by some condition of which we know nothing, and even the picturesque features of Dorsetshire landscape, that have always before dispersed his melancholy, fail to win his attention :

> Bright yellowhammers
> Made mirthful clamours,
> And billed long straws with a bustling air,
> And bearing their load,
> Flew up the road
> That he followed alone, without interest there.

The strongest of the poems of disillusion which are the outcome of this mood, is " The New-comer's Wife," with the terrible abruptness of its last stanza. It is not for criticism to find fault with the theme of a work of art, but only to comment upon its execution. Of the merit of these monotonously sinister *Satires of Circumstance* there can be no question ; whether the poet's in-dulgence in the mood which gave birth to them does not tend to lower our moral temperature and to lessen the rebound of our energy, is another matter. At all events, everyone must welcome a postscript in which a blast on the bugle of war seemed to have wakened the poet from his dark brooding to the sense of a new chapter in history.

In the fourth year of the war the veteran poet published *Moments of Vision*. These show a remarkable recovery of spirit, and an ingenuity never before excelled. With the passage of years Mr. Hardy, observing everything in the little world of Wessex, and forgetting nothing, has become almost preternaturally wise, and, if it may be said so, " knowing," with a sort of magic, like that of a wizard. He has learned to track the windings of the human heart with the familiarity of a game-keeper who finds plenty of vermin in the woods, and who nails what he finds, be it stoat or squirrel, to the barn-door of his poetry. But there is also in these last-fruits of Mr. Hardy's mossed tree much that is wholly detached from the bitterness of satire, much that simply records, with an infinite delicacy of pathos, little incidents of the personal life of long ago, bestowing the immortality of art on these fugitive fancies in the spirit of the Japanese sculptor when he chisels the melting of a cloud or the flight of an insect on his sword hilt :

> I idly cut a parsley stalk
> And blew therein towards the moon ;
> I had not thought what ghosts would walk
> With shivering footsteps to my tune.

THOMAS HARDY

I went and knelt, and scooped my hand
 As if to drink, into the brook,
And a faint figure seemed to stand
 Above me, with the bye-gone look.

I lipped rough rhymes of chance not choice,
 I thought not what my words might be ;
There came into my ear a voice
 That turned a tenderer verse for me.

We have now in brief historic survey marshalled
before us the various volumes in which Mr.
Hardy's lyrical poetry was originally collected.
Before we examine its general character more
closely, it may be well to call attention to its
technical quality, which was singularly misunderstood at first, and which has never, we believe,
been boldly faced. In 1898, and later, when a
melodious *falsetto* was much in fashion amongst
us, the reviewers found great fault with Mr.
Hardy's prosody : they judged him as a versifier
to be rude and incorrect. As regards the single
line, it may be confessed that Mr. Hardy, in his
anxiety to present his thought in an undiluted
form, is not infrequently clogged and hard. Such
a line as

 Fused from its separateness by ecstasy

hisses at us like a snake, and crawls like a wounded
one. Mr. Hardy is apt to clog his lines with con-
sonants, and he seems indifferent to the stiffness
which is the consequence of this neglect. Ben
Jonson said that "Donne, for not keeping of
accent, deserved hanging " ; perhaps we may go

so far as to say that Mr. Hardy, for his indifference
to a mellifluous run lays himself open to a mild
rebuke.   He is negligent of that eternal ornament
of English verse, audible intricacy, probably because of Swinburne's abuse of it.   But most of
what is called his harshness should rather be
called bareness, and is the result of a revolt, conscious or unconscious, against Keats's prescription
of " loading the rifts with ore."

In saying this, all has been said that an enemy
could in justice say in blame of his metrical
peculiarities.   Unquestionably he does occasionally, like Robert Browning, err in the direction of
cacophony.   But when we turn to the broader
part of prosody, we must perceive that Mr. Hardy
is not only a very ingenious, but a very correct
and admirable metricist.   His stanzaic invention
is abundant ; no other Victorian poet, not even
Swinburne, has employed so many forms, mostly
of his own invention, and employed them so
appropriately, that is to say, in so close harmony
with the subject or story enshrined in them.   To
take an example from his pure lyrics of reflection
first, from " The Bullfinches " :

> Brother Bulleys, let us sing
> From the dawn till evening !
> For we know not that we go not
> When the day's pale visions fold
> Unto those who sang of old,

in the exquisite fineness and sadness of the stanza
we seem to hear the very voices of the birds
warbling faintly in the sunset.   Again, the hurried,

238

timid irresolution of a lover always too late is marvellously rendered in the form of "Lizbie Browne":

> And Lizbie Browne,
> Who else had hair
> Bay-red as yours,
> Or flesh so fair
> Bred out of doors,
> Sweet Lizbie Browne?

On the other hand, the fierceness of "I said to Love" is interpreted in a stanza that suits the mood of denunciation, while "Tess's Lament" wails in a metre which seems to rock like an ageing woman seated alone before the fire, with an infinite haunting sadness.

It is, however, in the narrative pieces, the little *Wessex Tales*, that Mr. Hardy's metrical imagination is most triumphant. No two of these are identical in form, and for each he selects, or more often invents, a wholly appropriate stanza. He makes many experiments, one of the strangest being the introduction of rhymeless lines at regular intervals. Of this, "Cicely" is an example which repays attention:

> And still sadly onward I followed,
> That Highway the Icen
> Which trails its pale riband down Wessex
> O'er lynchet and lea.
>
> Along through the Stour-bordered Forum,
> Where legions had wayfared,
> And where the slow river up-glasses
> Its green canopy;

and one still more remarkable is the enchanting " Friends Beyond," to which we shall presently recur. The drawling voice of a weary old campaigner is wonderfully rendered in the stanza of " Valenciennes " :

> Well : Heaven wi' its jasper halls
> Is now the on'y town I care to be in . . .
> Good Lord, if Nick should bomb the walls
> As we did Valencieën !

whereas for long Napoleonic stories like " Leipzig " and " The Peasant's Confession," a balladmeasure which contemporaries such as Southey or Campbell might have used is artfully chosen. In striking contrast we have the elaborate verseform of " The Souls of the Slain," in which the throbbing stanza seems to dilate and withdraw like the very cloud of moth-like phantoms which it describes. It is difficult to follow out this theme without more frequent quotation than I have space for here, but the reader who pursues it carefully will not repeat the rumour that Mr. Hardy is a careless or " incorrect " metricist. He is, on the contrary, a metrical artist of great accomplishment.

The conception of life revealed in his verses by this careful artist is one which displays very exactly the bent of his temperament. During the whole of his long career Mr. Hardy has not budged an inch from his original line of direction. He holds that, abandoned by God, treated with scorn by Nature, man lies helpless at the mercy of " those purblind

Doomsters," accident, chance, and time, from whom he has had to endure injury and insult from the cradle to the grave. This is stating the Hardy doctrine in its extreme form, but it is not stating it too strongly. This has been called his " pessimism," a phrase to which some admirers, unwilling to give things their true name, have objected. But, of course, Mr. Hardy is a pessimist, just as Browning is an optimist, just as white is not black, and day is not night. Our juggling with words in paradox is too often apt to disguise a want of decision in thought. Let us admit that Mr. Hardy's conception of the fatal forces which beleaguer human life is a " pessimistic " one, or else words have no meaning.

Yet it is needful to define in what this pessimism consists. It is not the egotism of Byron or the morbid melancholy of Chateaubriand. It is directed towards an observation of others, not towards an analysis of self, and this gives it more philosophical importance, because although romantic peevishness is very common among modern poets, and although ennui inspires a multitude of sonnets, a deliberate and imaginative study of useless suffering in the world around us is rare indeed among the poets. It is particularly to be noted that Mr. Hardy, although one of the most profoundly tragic of all modern writers, is neither effeminate nor sickly. His melancholy could never have dictated the third stanza of Shelley's " Lines written in Dejection in the Bay of Naples." His pessimism is involuntary, forced from him by his experience and his constitution, and no analysis could give a better definition of what divides him from the petulant despair of a poet like Leopardi than the lines " To Life " :

O life, with the sad scared face,
      I weary of seeing thee,
And thy draggled cloak, and thy hobbling pace,
      And thy too-forced pleasantry !

I know what thou would'st tell
      Of Death, Time, Destiny—
I have known it long, and know, too, well
      What it all means for me.

But canst thou not array
      Thyself in rare disguise,
And feign like truth, for one mad day,
      That Earth is Paradise ?

I'll tune me to the mood,
      And mumm with thee till eve,
And maybe what as interlude
      I feign, I shall believe !

But the mumming goes no deeper than it does in the exquisite poem of " The Darkling Thrush," where the carolings of an aged bird, on a frosty evening, are so ecstatic that they waken a vague hope in the listener's mind that the thrush may possibly know of " some blessed hope " of which the poet is " unaware." This is as far as Mr. Hardy ever gets on the blest Victorian pathway of satisfaction.

There are certain aspects in which it is not

unnatural to see a parallel between Mr. Hardy and
George Crabbe. Each is the spokesman of a
district, each has a passion for the study of mankind, each has gained by long years of observation
a profound knowledge of local human character,
and each has plucked on the open moor, and wears
in his coat, the hueless flower of disillusion. But
there is a great distinction in the aim of the two
poets. Crabbe, as he describes himself in *The
Parish Register*, was " the true physician " who
" walks the foulest ward." He was utilitarian in
his morality; he exposed the pathos of tragedy by
dwelling on the faults which led to it, forgetful
of the fatality which in more consistent moments
he acknowledged. Crabbe was realistic with a
moral design, even in the *Tales of the Hall*, where
he made a gallant effort at last to arrive at a de-
tachment of spirit. No such effort is needed by
Mr. Hardy, who has none of the instinct of a
preacher, and who considers moral improvement
outside his responsibility. He admits, with his
great French contemporary, that

> Tout désir est menteur, toute joie éphémère,
> Toute liqueur au fond de la coupe est amère,

but he is bent on discovering the cause of this
devastation, and not disposed to waste time over
its consequences. At the end he produces a
panacea which neither Crabbe nor Byron dreamed
of—resignation.

But the poet has not reached the end of his
disillusion. He thinks to secure repose on the

breast of Nature, the *alma mater*, to whom Goethe
and Wordsworth and Browning each in his own
way turned, and were rewarded by consolation
and refreshment. We should be prepared to find
Mr. Hardy, with his remarkable aptitude for the
perception of natural forms, easily consoled by the
influences of landscape and the inanimate world.
His range of vision is wide and extremely exact ;
he has the gift of reproducing before us scenes
of various character with a vividness which is
sometimes startling. But Mr. Hardy's disdain of
sentimentality, and his vigorous analysis of the
facts of life, render him insensible not indeed to
he mysttery nor to the beauty, but to the imagined
sympathy, of Nature. He has no more confidence
in the visible earth than in the invisible heavens,
and neither here nor there is he able to persuade
himself to discover a counsellor or a friend. In
this connection we do well to follow the poet's
train of thought in the lyric called " In a Wood,"
where he enters a copse dreaming that, in that
realm of " sylvan peace," Nature would offer
" a soft release from man's unrest." He immediately observes that the pine and the beech
are struggling for existence, and trying to blight
each other with dripping poison. He sees the ivy
eager to strangle the elm, and the hawthorns
choking the hollies. Even the poplars sulk and
turn black under the shadow of a rival. In the
end, filled with horror at all these crimes of Nature,
the poet flees from the copse as from an accursed
place, and he determines that life offers him no

consolation except the company of those human
beings who are as beleaguered as himself :

> Since, then, no grace I find
>   Taught me of trees,
> Turn I back to my kind
>   Worthy as these.
> There at least smiles abound,
> There discourse trills around,
> There, now and then, are found,
>   Life-loyalties.

It is absurd, he decides, to love Nature, which
has either no response to give, or answers in
irony.   Let us even avoid, as much as we can, deep
concentration of thought upon the mysteries of
Nature, lest we become demoralised by contemplat-
ing her negligence, her blindness, her implacability.
We find here a violent reaction against the poetry
of egotistic optimism which had ruled the romantic
school in England for more than a hundred years,
and we recognise a branch of Mr. Hardy's
originality.   He has lifted the veil of Isis, and he
finds beneath it, not a benevolent mother of men,
but the tomb of an illusion.   One short lyric,
" Yell'ham-Wood's Story", puts this, again with
a sylvan setting, in its unflinching crudity :

> Coomb-Firtrees say that Life is a moan,
>   And Clyffe-hill Clump says " Yea ! "
> But Yell'ham says a thing of its own :
>   It's not, " Gray, gray,
>   Is Life alway ! "
>   That Yell'ham says,
> Nor that Life is for ends unknown.

It says that Life would signify
A thwarted purposing :
That we come to live, and are called to die.
Yes, that's the thing
In fall, in spring,
That Yell'ham says :—
" Life offers—to deny ! "

It is therefore almost exclusively to the obscure history of those who suffer and stumble around him, victims of the universal disillusion, men and women " come to live but called to die," that Mr. Hardy dedicates his poetic function. " Lizbie Browne " appeals to us as a typical instance of his rustic pathos, his direct and poignant tenderness, and if we compare it with such poems of Wordsworth's as " Lucy Gray " or " Alice Fell " we see that he starts by standing much closer to the level of the subject than his great predecessor does. Wordsworth is the benevolent philosopher sitting in a post - chaise or crossing the " wide moor " in meditation. Mr. Hardy is the familiar neighbour, the shy mourner at the grave ; his relation is a more intimate one: he is patient, humble, un-upbraiding. Sometimes, as in the remarkable colloquy called " The Ruined Maid," his sympathy is so close as to offer an absolute flout in the face to the system of Victorian morality. Mr. Hardy, indeed, is not concerned with sentimental morals, but with the primitive instincts of the soul, applauding them, or at least recording them with complacency, even when they outrage ethical tradition, as they do in the lyric narrative called "A Wife and Another."

246

The stanzas " To an Unborn Pauper Child "
sum up what is sinister and what is genial in Mr.
Hardy's attitude to the unambitious forms of life
which he loves to contemplate.

His temperature is not always so low as it is in
the class of poems to which we have just referred,
but his ultimate view is never more sanguine. He
is pleased sometimes to act as the fiddler at a dance,
surveying the hot - blooded couples, and urging
them on by the lilt of his instrument, but he is
always perfectly aware that they will have " to
pay high for their prancing " at the end of all.
No instance of this is more remarkable than the
poem called " Julie-Jane," a perfect example of
Mr. Hardy's metrical ingenuity and skill, which
begins thus :

> Sing ; how 'a would sing !
> How 'a would raise the tune
> When we rode in the waggon from harvesting
> By the light o' the moon !
>
> Dance ; how 'a would dance !
> If a fiddlestring did but sound
> She would hold out her coats, give a slanting glance,
> And go round and round.
>
> Laugh ; how 'a would laugh !
> Her peony lips would part
> As if none such a place for a lover to quaff
> At the deeps of a heart,

and which then turns to the most plaintive and the
most irreparable tragedy, woven, as a black design
on to a background of gold, upon this basis of
temperamental joyousness.

Alphonse Daudet once said that the great gift of Edmond de Goncourt was to "*rendre l'irrendable*." This is much more true of Mr. Hardy than it was of Goncourt, and more true than it is of any other English poet except Donne. There is absolutely no observation too minute, no flutter of reminiscence too faint, for Mr. Hardy to adopt as the subject of a metaphysical lyric, and his skill in this direction has grown upon him ; it is nowhere so remarkable as in his latest volume, aptly termed *Moments of Vision*. Everything in village life is grist to his mill ; he seems to make no selection, and his field is modest to humility and yet practically boundless. We have a poem on the attitude of two people with nothing to do and no book to read, waiting in the parlour of an hotel for the rain to stop, a recollection after more than forty years. That the poet once dropped a pencil into the cranny of an old church where he was sketching inspires an elaborate lyric. The disappearance of a rotted summer-house, the look of a row of silver drops of fog condensed on the bar of a gate, the effect of candlelight years and years ago on a woman's neck and hair, the vision of a giant at a fair, led by a dwarf with a red string—such are amongst the subjects which awaken in Mr. Hardy thoughts which do often lie too deep for tears, and call for interpretation in verse. The skeleton of a lady's sunshade, picked up on Swanage Cliffs, the pages of a fly-blown Testament lying in a railway waiting-room, a journeying boy in a third-class carriage, with his ticket stuck in the band of his hat—such are among the themes which awake in Mr. Hardy's imagination reveries which are always wholly serious and usually deeply tragic.

Mr. Hardy's notation of human touches hitherto excluded from the realm of poetry is one of the most notable features of his originality. It marked his work from the beginning, as in the early ballad of " The Widow," where the sudden damping of the wooer's amatory ardour in consequence of his jealousy of the child is rendered with extraordinary refinement. The difficulty of course is to know when to stop. There is always a danger that a poet, in his search after the infinitely ingenious, may lapse into *amphigory*, into sheer absurdity and triviality, which Cowper, in spite of his elegant lightness, does not always escape. Wordsworth, more serious in his intent, fell headlong in parts of " Peter Bell," and in such ballads as " Betty Foy." Mr. Hardy, whatever the poverty of his incident, commonly redeems it by the oddity of his observation ; as in " The Pedigree " :

> I bent in the deep of night
> Over a pedigree the chronicler gave
> As mine ; and as I bent there, half-unrobed,
> The uncurtained panes of my window-square
> Let in the watery light
> Of the moon in its old age :
> And green-rheumed clouds were hurrying past
> Where mute and cold it globed
> Like a dying dolphin's eye seen through a lapping wave.

Mr. Hardy's love of strange experiences, and of adventures founded on a balance of conscience and instinct, is constantly exemplified in those ballads and verse - anecdotes which form the section of his poetry most appreciated by the general public. Among these, extraordinarily representative of the poet's habit of mind, is " My Cicely," a tale of the eighteenth century, where a man impetuously rides from London through Wessex to be present at the funeral of the wrong woman ; as he returns, by a coincidence, he meets the right woman, whom he used to love, and is horrified at " her liquor - fired face, her thick accents." He determines that by an effort of will the dead woman (whom he never saw) shall remain, what she seemed during his wild ride, " *my* Cicely," and the living woman be expunged from memory. A similar deliberate electing that the dream shall hold the place of the fact is the motive of " The Well - Beloved." The ghastly humour of " The Curate's Kindness " is a sort of reverse action of the same mental subtlety. Misunderstanding takes a very prominent place in Mr. Hardy's irony of circumstance ; as, almost too painfully, in " The Rash Bride," a hideous tale of suicide following on the duplicity of a tender and innocent widow.

The grandmother of Mr. Hardy was born in 1772, and survived until 1857. From her lips he heard many an obscure old legend of the life of Wessex in the eighteenth century. Was it she who told him the terrible Exmoor story of " The Sacrilege " ; the early tale of " The Two Men," which might be the skeleton-scenario for a whole elaborate novel; or that incomparable comedy in verse, " The Fire at Tranter Sweatley's," with its splendid human touch at the very end ? We suspect that it was; and perhaps at the same source he acquired his dangerous insight into the female heart, whether exquisitely feeble as in " The Home-coming," with its delicate and ironic surprise, or treacherous, as in the desolating ballad of " Rose-Ann." No one, in prose or verse, has expatiated more poignantly than Mr. Hardy on what our forefathers used to call " cases of conscience." He seems to have shared the experiences of souls to whom life was " a wood before your doors, and a labyrinth within the wood, and locks and bars to every door within that labyrinth," as Jeremy Taylor describes that of the anxious penitents who came to him to confession. The probably very early story of " The Caster-bridge Captains " is a delicate study in com-punction, and a still more important example is " The Alarm," where the balance of conscience and instinct gives to what in coarser hands might seem the most trivial of actions a momentous character of tragedy.

This is one of Mr. Hardy's studies in military history, where he is almost always singularly happy. His portraits of the non - commissioned officer of the old service are as excellent in verse as they are in the prose of *The Trumpet-Major* or *The Melancholy Hussar*. The reader of the novels will not have to be reminded that " Valen-ciennes " and the other ballads have their prose-parallel in Simon Burden's reminiscences of Minden. Mr. Hardy, with a great curiosity about the science of war and a close acquaintance with the mind of the common soldier, has pondered on the philosophy of fighting. " The Man he Killed," written in 1902, expresses the wonder of the rifleman who is called upon to shoot his brother-in-arms, although

> Had he and I but met,
> By some old ancient inn,
> We should have set us down to wet
> Right many a nipperkin.

In this connection the *Poems of War and Patriotism*, which form an important part of the volume of 1918, should be carefully examined by those who meditate on the tremendous problems of the moment.

A poet so profoundly absorbed in the study of life could not fail to speculate on the probabilities of immortality. Here Mr. Hardy presents to us his habitual serenity in negation. He sees the beautiful human body " lined by tool of time," and he asks what becomes of it when its dissolution is complete. He sees no evidence of a conscious state after death, of what would have to be, in the case of aged or exhausted persons, a revival of spiritual force, and on the whole he is disinclined to cling to the faith in a future life. He holds that the immortality of a dead man resides in the memory of the living, his " finer part shining within ever-faithful hearts of those bereft." He pursues this theme in a large number of his most serious and affecting lyrics, most gravely perhaps in " The To-be-Forgotten " and in " The Superseded." This sense of the forlorn condition of the dead, surviving only in the dwindling memory of the living, inspires what has some claims to be considered the loveliest of all Mr. Hardy's poems, " Friends Beyond," which in its tenderness, its humour, and its pathos contains in a few pages every characteristic of his genius.

His speculation perceives the dead as a crowd of slowly vanishing phantoms, clustering in their ineffectual longing round the footsteps of those through whom alone they continue to exist. This conception has inspired Mr. Hardy with several wonderful visions, among which the spectacle of " The Souls of the Slain " in the Boer War, alighting like vast flights of moths, over Portland Bill at night, is the most remarkable. It has the sublimity and much of the character of some apocalyptic design by Blake. The volume of 1902 contains a whole group of phantasmal pieces of this kind, where there is frequent mention of spectres, who address the poet in the accents of nature, as in the unrhymed ode called " The Mother Mourns." The obsession of old age, with its physical decay (" I look into my glass "), the inevitable division which leads to that isolation which the poet regards as the greatest of adversities (" The Impercipient "), the tragedies of moral indecision, the contrast between the tangible earth and the bodyless ghosts, and endless repetition of the cry, " Why find we us here ? " and of the question " Has some Vast Imbecility framed us in jest, and left us now to hazardry ? "—all start from the overwhelming love of physical life and acquaintance with its possibilities, which Mr. Hardy possesses to an inordinate degree.

It would be ridiculous at the close of an essay to attempt any discussion of the huge dramatic panorama which many believe to be Mr. Hardy's most weighty contribution to English literature. The spacious theatre of *The Dynasts* with its comprehensive and yet concise realisations of vast passages of human history, is a work which calls for a commentary as lengthy as itself, and yet needs no commentary at all. No work of the imagination is more its own interpreter than this sublime historic peep-show, this rolling vision of the Napoleonic chronicle drawn on the broadest lines, and yet in detail made up of intensely concentrated and vivid glimpses of reality. But the subject of my present study, the lyrical poetry of Mr. Hardy, is not largely illustrated in *The Dynasts*, except by the choral interludes of the phantom intelligences, which have great lyrical value, and by three or four admirable songs.

When we resume the effect which the poetry of Mr. Hardy makes upon the careful reader, we note, as I have indicated already, a sense of unity of direction throughout. Mr. Hardy has expressed himself in a thousand ways, but has never altered his vision. From 1867 to 1917, through half a century of imaginative creation, he has not modified the large outlines of his art in the smallest degree. To early readers of his poems, before the full meaning of them became evident, his voice sounded inharmonious, because it did not fit in with the exquisite melodies of the later Victorian age. But Mr. Hardy, with characteristic pertinacity, did not attempt to alter his utterance in the least, and now we can all perceive, if we take the trouble to do so, that what seemed harsh in his poetry was his peculiar and personal mode of interpreting his thoughts to the world.

As in his novels so in his poems, Mr. Hardy has chosen to remain local, to be the interpreter for present and future times of one rich and neglected province of the British realm. From his standpoint there he contemplates the wide aspect of life, but it seems huge and misty to him, and he broods over the tiny incidents of Wessex idiosyncrasy. His irony is audacious and even sardonic, and few poets have been less solicitous to please their weaker brethren. But no poet of modern times has been more careful to avoid the abstract and to touch upon the real.